THE FIRST 60 YEARS

THE HISTORY OF AFRO-AMERICAN MUSICAL THEATER AND ENTERTAINMENT 1865-1930

Ronald Smokey Stevens

Gloria thank you 3x
For allowing my voice
To Be Heard

Smokey Stevens
2012

Avid Readers Publishing Group
Lakewood, California

The opinions expressed in this manuscript are those of the author and do not represent the thoughts or opinions of the publisher. The author in no way claims ownership to any of the historical information contained in this book. This history belongs to those who lived it and made it.

THE FIRST 60 YEARS

All Rights Reserved

Copyright © 2013 Ronald Smokey Stevens

Avid Readers Publishing Group

http://www.avidreaderspg.com

ISBN-13:978-1-61286-189-0

For Speaking Engagements and Bookings

Contact----3 E Productions

email--t3eprod@yahoo.com

shobiz4u@verizon.net

Printed in the United States

MY JOURNEY TO THIS DISCOVERY

My first exposure to my entertainment history occurred when I performed in my first BROADWAY production: "BUBBLING BROWN SUGAR." I knew about the black writers of the past like Langston Hughes, Zora Neele Hurston, W.E.B. Dubois, and others through my training at The D.C. Black Repertory Company. However, in this production I got the opportunity to meet, work, and become friends with my living history. AVON LONG, CHARLES HONI COLES, CAB CALLOWAY, JIMMY CROSS, of "STUMP & STUMPY" fame, and MR. COOKIE of "COOK & BROWN, just to name a few.

"BUBBLING BROWN SUGAR," paid a tribute to the contributions made by black artists during "The Harlem Rennansaince," of the 1920's. However, it was "HONI COLES," that took me under his wing, taught me all of those historic tap routines, and educated me about our musical theater history. I talked, listened, and drank with him for over a year and a half listening to his stories and reminiscing about our history that he was all too willing to share with me. "BUBBLING BROWN SUGAR" eventually closed, but the seed was planted. I hung on to all the material I was exposed to in "Bubbling." 1985 I co-conceived, choreographed, and performed in my production entitled "SHOOT ME WHILE I'M HAPPY," at The Victory Gardens Theater in Chicago, written by playwrite STEVE CARTER. In 1987 my late friend and I conceived, wrote, produced and performed in our production entitled "ROLLIN' with STEVENS & STEWART," A Tribute To The Last Days of Black Vaudeville, which was performed nationwide for over seven years.

In 1998 I found producers in New York City and changed the name to "ROLLIN' on THE T.O.B.A'. It was

iii

first produced at The Intar Theater on 42nd St. It then moved off Broadway to the 47th St. Theater, to rave reviews, before moving on BROADWAY to The Henry Miller Theater.

Unfortunately, my delightful, enlightening, historic, as well as entertaining, BROADWAY show was totally short lived. However because of the history contained in my show, it was suggested to me on many occasions that I should write a book on the subject and period. I took up the challenge and this is the result of my efforts. Finally had I had more information when I renamed my show "ROLLIN on THE TOBA," It might have been called "ROLLIN On THE DUDLEY CIRCUIT" instead, and after you read this book you will soon understand why……..

Ronald Smokey Stevens

THE 1st 60 YEARS
THE HISTORY OF AFRO-AMERICAN MUSICAL THEATER AND ENTERTAINMENT
1865-1930

As we focus on the period of Afro-American musical theater from 1865 through the 1920's, the period during and after minstrelsy, the period before radio and during the development of silent films the talkies or movies, it is imperative that we look at the minstrel period in American entertainment, which began in the 1840's.

During this 'minstrel period,' white performers exploited on stage the inhumane living conditions of African American slaves for their amusement. They did this through "coon songs," soft shoe dancing, simple jokes, slap-stick behavior, and their infamous trademark, "the burnt cork or black face makeup."

These white minstrel shows gained wide popularity as they traveled the country and performed for U.S. presidents by stereotyping and creating, a non-thinking, shuffling, ignorant black character for everyone's amusement. This type of buffoonery and false imagery of African Americans on stage was the beginnings of American musical theater and entertainment, which lasted for over 50 years.

Ronald Smokey Stevens

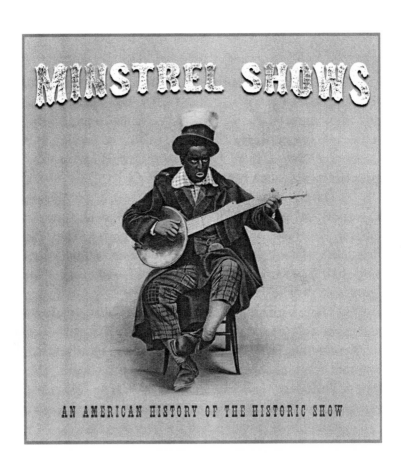

MINSTREL SHOWS

AN AMERICAN HISTORY OF THE HISTORIC SHOW

However, African Americans did not enter into this playing arena until the close of the civil war. These Afro-American minstrel performers were able to capitalize on white America's fascination with their culture. Against the violent backdrop following the civil war, Charles Hicks, a black man, was able to organize the first successful black-owned minstrel company in 1865: The Georgia Minstrels. Forming the company in Cincinnati, Ohio, the troupe was able to travel throughout the U.S. before traveling to Germany, in doing so, establishing Black Minstrelsy.

Georgia Minstrels

This was the first example of black entertainment entrepreneurship, and contrary to historical beliefs, these first black minstrels did not perform in the traditional "blackface." With a nation interested in seeing "the genuine negro," these Afro-American performers elected not to blacken their face.

"Unlike white minstrel performers, the first black minstrels did not
blacken-up, and the audience were often
astonished to see ex-slaves having a
range of skin color from almost white, to
ebony black. The troupes that "Hicks and
McAdoo," took to Australia in the 1890's
also did not perform in black-face (THE
GHOST WALKS, pg. 283)."

Yet blackface was not completely absent from black minstrelsy. Many of the comedians of that era elected to blacken their faces to distinguish between the "straight man" and the jokester. Also the blackface, coupled with the comedian's outlandish clothes, added to his comic ensemble.

While some comedians of the period, such as Bert Williams, S. H. Dudley, Salem Tutt Whitney, and Tom McIntosh, performed in "blackface," most did not, including Bob Cole, and Billy Kersands.

Black Minstrelsy came in two unique categories: tent shows, a carryover from an earlier period, and Legitimate Minstrel Shows, more or less an imitation of white minstrel shows. The blues got its exposure and a foothold in show business due to tent shows. Black tent shows were designed for blacks

.......but you couldn't keep whites out. They came to steal material or just to be entertained.

The tent show was part circus, part theater, and part minstrel show. There were clowns, acrobats, theatrical sketches, musical numbers, marching displays, all under one tent.

The show usually started at 7pm. and lasted well into the night. A curtain was erected, which either rose and fell like a shade, or parted in the middle. The troupe curtain was the object of much concern and superstition. It was carried from town to town.

Ma Rainey was Queen of the colored tent shows in the rural South. She and her husband, Pa Rainey, were the creators of "The Rabbit Foot Minstrels" (circa 1880's). Ma Rainey even discovered Bessie Smith, who traveled with Ma Rainey in the early days. When Ma Rainey became more successful, she even owned her own railroad cars, one for her, and the other for the show members. They went on to create "Pa Rainey's Minstrels," and in 1915 "Rainey and Rainey" the Assinators of the Blues, another first of black entertainment entrepreneurialism.

Ma Rainey

There were other black entrepreneurs of the period that created minstrel companies: "Hicks and Sawyer Minstrels," "The Richards and Pringle Minstrels," "McCabe and Young Minstrels," "The Mahara Minstrels," as well as "The Billy Kersands Minstrels."

"Black Patti's Troubadors" was an important minstrel show and outfit organized in 1895. Mme Sisseretta Jones, "The Black Patti," was an astute business woman and an awesome singer with an operatic voice that had a very wide range. Her specialty was to sing a chorus in one range and then sing the same chorus in an octave higher. Her troupe traveled the U.S. and Europe for many years, from 1895 through 1920, discovering new talent and providing jobs for many Afro-American performers, while many black people struggled to eke out an existence, only 30 yrs after being emancipated from slavery.

These are a well-dressed group of four automaton figures, which on being wound up go through a variety of entertaining life-like movements, in imitation of playing the Banjo, Bones, Tambourine etc., while the old lady fans herself vigorously and smiles approval to effect is irresi   comical.

8

Legitimate black minstrel shows were close imitations of white minstrel pattern shows. A hall or theater would be rented, notices would be posted, sometimes well in advance. The show would open with the minstrels marching in to a nifty "cakewalk" or "two step." There was always some fancy footwork involved, and the music was "hot." Dixie Land Jazz and Rag Time were the direct descendants of black minstrel march music. James Rosamond Johnson, W.C. Handy, and James A. Bland wrote high stepping march numbers for minstrel bands.

"White minstrelsy was, on the whole, a caricature of Negro life, and it fixed a stage tradition, which has not been entirely broken. It fixed the tradition of the Negro as only an irresponsible, happy-go-lucky, wide grinning, loud laughing, shuffling, banjo playing, singing and dancing sort of being. Nevertheless these companies did provide an essential stage training and theatrical experience which at the time could not have been acquired from any other source (James Weldon Johnson, Black Manhattan, pg. 2).

It is extremely important to understand that this medium, minstrelsy, also allowed black men and women the opportunity to become and grow as entrepreneurs for the first time in our history during a time when a "black businessman or woman was unheard of and rarely accepted.

THE BREAK FROM MINSTRELSY

Longing to embrace a performance void of exaggerated caricatures of Afro-American life to celebrate the beauty was found in "THE CREOLE SHOW," created by esteemed black actor, Sam Lucas, and Sam T. Jack, successful theater owner in 1891. This show was the first show to depart from the minstrel format, and it opened a floodgate for a host of black musical theater and comedy. It was the first of its kind to present a beautiful female chorus to eager audiences. It opened in Boston during The World's Fair of 1891and later moved to New York's Standard Theater. The show experienced a long life filled with raving reviews.

> "Sam T. Jack and Sam Lucas Creole Burlesque Company recently opened at The London Theater, NYC. The show commenced with a very pretty first part, an attractive groupings of shapely femininity." The olio sketches were very fine and called for numerous encores. The burlesque "The beauty of the Nile, by William Wait was fine (*Indianapolis Freeman*, September 20, 1891)."

Bob Cole, a 26 yr old Afro-American performer (who performed in The Creole Show), continued to push the door open for the departure from minstrelsy around 1897 with the development of "the resident stock company." As organizer of the first resident stock company, Mr. Cole broke the minstrel mode entirely. Mr. Cole embraced the art of formal theatrical training with zeal and vigor. He served as the company's playwright and stage manager because of his creative ingenuity. The company, composed of 12 to 15 members, was anxious to test this new field of study and creativity in their community. They performed in this new genre beautifully. The resident stock company threw away the caricatures and grossly exaggerated performances in exchange for a more sophisticated performance. These stock performers began to stretch their creative wings to include dramas, comedies, farce comedies, as well as musicals.

As a result of this new genre, there began a great demand for stock companies, especially in the South. Because of the large African American population in the South, they provided great support for the stock company performances in spite of the living conditions. Coupled with the construction of Afro-American theaters, the South became a performers' paradise. The rapid construction of black theaters in the South between 1916 and 1921 also made it possible for these shows to make several appearances in one city and reduce the traveling time between cities that were able to accommodate them. In addition, several theaters, including The Howard in D.C., The Grand in Chicago, as well as The Lafayette in N.Y.C., had resident stock companies which put on original shows on a weekly basis.

Theater owners were eager for the stock performers to extend their performances because of their attraction and financial success. In return, they were able to pay their performers good salaries. Typical salaries ranged from $5 a week for the chorus girls and between $20 and $35 a week for the principals. Yet the experience received by a performer in a stock company under a good director and producer was invaluable. The members of the company were required to be versatile and self-reliant. From this strenuous training, the performers were able to successfully enter almost any department of theatrical endeavor. Some noted black stock companies were "The Stevens & Williams Co," "The George Freeman Co.," "The Billy King Stock

Co," and "The Sidney Perrin's Co."

"The Pekin Stock Company created by Robert Motts, owner of the Pekin Theater in Chicago, gained unsurpassed success in 1906. Shortly after Motts opened his theater, several whites opened theaters in close proximity to his, which also catered to black audiences. Fighting fierce competition, Motts demanded excellence and powerful creativity from his stock company. With over 20 artists, Motts presented new plays every two weeks, presenting fresh talent and new and exciting performances for his enormous audiences.

> "The Pekin with its talented stock company quickly became the "Mecca" of black entertainment. Almost all of the black stars of the period played The Pekins, and it became a major tourist attraction (*Blacks in Blackface*-pg. 280)."

In April, 1908, Marion A. Brooks and Flournoy Miller took a dozen or more players from Chicago to Montgomery, Alabama for the establishing of a stock company at the newly opened

Bijou Theater. The company, "The Bijou Stock Co." was one of the first black theaters in the South.

Another stock company that gained notoriety was The Negro Players of The Lafayette Theater in N.Y.C. in 1912. Under the direction of Marion Cook, this stock company performed dramatic pieces as well as comedies and musicals. This stock company set in place a dramatic training ground for the first few years until the actors could perform their entire repertoire.

"The Negro Players, a company formed for the development of Negro music and drama, will open at the Lafayette Theater, a large theater located in Harlem, on March 17, a series of productions. The founders of the organization aim to put into characterization a music and dramatic form, real pictures of Negro life both in city and plantation (*The New York Age*, 1913)."

Bob Cole

With the success of the stock company and the newfound performance freedom, Bob Cole wanted to test the water further by producing his first show, "A Trip to Coontown," which strayed totally away from the outdated minstrel format. Produced in 1897 by Bob Cole and Billy Johnson, this performance shocked the theater community, as it was the first musical featuring an all black cast and was the first show to be written, produced, managed, and staged by blacks. However, more importantly, "A Trip to Coontown," unlike any other production with African American performers, contained a continuity line with characters working out the story from beginning to end.

This was the first step in the total abandonment of the minstrel shows. The show opened on September 27, 1897, at South Amboy, New Jersey. Its New York performances were at Miner's Eighth Ave Theater, and because of its success it eventually moved to the Grand Opera House and Casino Roof.

"A Trip to Coontown" brought together some of the greatest creative African American artists of the time. However, this powerful production was not exempt from its own controversy. One of the celebrated poets of the era, Paul Lawrence Dunbar, had an idea for a comic opera, which closely resembled "A Trip to Coontown."

"Paul Lawrence Dunbar, the Negro poet, who announced the other day that he was about to collaborate with James Whitcomb and write a comic opera for Negro actors, has been anticipated. At the Third St. Theater this week Cole and Johnson's select company is appearing in "A Trip to Coontown" and the plot of the piece bars quite a resemblance to the story which Mr. Dunbar has laid out for his comic opera. This, mind you, is no charge of plagiarism, for the idea of the scalawag who poses himself for a prince was very popular in those days before Mr. Dunbar was born. At the Third Ave. Theater, however, the idea has been used to fine advantage, and the result is one of the most artistic farce comedy shows that New York has seen in a long time. There is a many white comedian who could sit at the feet of these Negro

actors, and learn a thing or two (New York,NY
April 16, 1898)."

"A Trip to Coontown" was not immune to the
racism and prejudices in America as well. On one such
occasion, the production was slowed down because of
white musicians refusing to play with African American
band members.

"A Trip to Coontown," played to fair
houses last week while exhibiting in this city.
During the first part of the week the company
was considerably hampered by the prejudiced
white musicians who refused to play with the
company's colored orchestra leader. The uncalled
for prejudice was overruled however, and the last
part of the week found the colored men leading,
and the company doing hot work (Feb 18, 1899,
The Indianapolis Freeman).

As "A Trip to Coontown" broke away from the
old minstrel format, there was, however, some residual
carryover from that period. Even the names "coon" and
"nigger" were being used in shows and songs about African
Americans to the distaste of the community at large. During
that period, all reviews written about black musicals and
shows were written by whites from a white perspective.
However, Sylvester Russell, a frustrated singer, began
writing reviews of black performers which appeared in
the Indianapolis Freeman and other black weeklies. These
papers were read by many in the entertainment industry.
His theatrical criticism covering black entertainment is
probably the most extensive of the period. Russell was
also the first to speak out strongly in print against the then

common use of the words "nigger" and "coon" in popular songs.

Dating back from publication of a song called "Nigger Never Die," which was significantly enough sung in the most prominent minstrel companies in America, I have found it quite necessary to call the attention of song publishers to the fact that all the nations are now being represented in the popular song business, and the time is here when each race of people whose way of life is set to music is looking eagerly at the publishers to see what advantage they are permitting song writers to take of the caricature of their race. They are interested to see if it is pure fun or common insult. William Jerome, a very prolific writer, who composed such a beautiful compliment to the Irish race as "Bedelia," is the man whose later production of a coon song, "Why Don't You Go Go Go," inspired me to write this article. Mr. Jerome has used the words, "common nigger," in his song. In taking exception to this low degrading word, which does not apply to the Negro race at all, I wish to remind the popular intelligent song publishers in America, and especially in New York where intelligence is above all things, that the Irish race of people are more sensitive than any other race, and for this reason their race has been treated with great precaution by the modern songwriters of today. The publishers, many of them Hebrews, take care that the word, "sheenee," does not go to press. The Italians are also favored, and the word "dago" is prohibited. Recently we had a Negro songwriter in Chicago who wrote a song with the word "nigger" in it, but the actors of his race will never sing it. Futhermore, we admit he is just as ignorant as his white counterparts. The modern school of distinguished, educated colored songwriters without complaint has set a new example, and all the most intelligent in America are now singing their songs. Among these writers are Bob Cole, J. Rosemond Johnson, Sidney

Perrin, Billy Johnson, Nathan Bibins, Al Johns, Shepard Edmonds, Bill Hammer, Will Tobias, and others. The sense and substance of the matter is this: The Negro race has no objections to the word, coon, and no objections to the word, "darkie." We care nothing for the words black, or colored, or Negro. But we totally object to the word "nigger." We are the race of people that is continually insulted by the common people without complaint. Why should not the word "nigger be abolished?" I will remind all concerned of the fact that this word has appeared in the late songs mostly from the pens of Irish and Jewish writers. As an ignorant Negro, I must further remind you all of two racial facts in the history of these two races.

The American Jews have suffered from American prejudice, the successful Jews, regardless of this fact, are not affected with race prejudice. The Irish as it shows by their daily history, are the most prejudiced race of all, taught to them in their homes and through popular songs. How sad that when we think that under these circumstances, the men who write these songs will continue to teach the low element of the world to call us nigger. Colored song writers have never insulted any of the white races. Why then should the song publishers accept a manuscript that would insult the colored race? Now is the time for us to tell every race under the sun, just for fun, that we do not care for anymore ignorant display of the word nigger from chumps of songwriters, unfair publishers and stage performers (Sylvester Russell, *Indianapolis Freeman* 1905).

In an interview with Bob Cole the creator of "A Trip to Coontown," the issue of the usage of the word "coon" in popular music is addressed:

"The word coon is very insulting and must be soon eliminated. You have crusaded against the word nigger, Mr. Russell, and now I'm going to crusade against the word coon. The best class of white people in America abhors the word coon and feel ashamed whenever they hear it used. In London, we had found it used in common slander.

Mr. Cole was asked why....several years ago he had named his comedy "A Trip to Coontown"....? Cole replied, "that the day had passed with the flowing tide of revealations." He added that even the titles "jungles" and "hottest coon" should be set aside. He said that "Williams & Walker" should not have used their card titled "Two Real Coons", in Europe and should drop it forever. Cole also said how the Irish will not stand for the "mike" and how "Sheenee" and "dago" are ruled out. He said there is no harm in the word Negro, darkie, colored, or Afro-american. He related with disgust how the compilers of the new American Standard Dictionary have the ill breeding to give the definition of "coon" as a relative of the colored race.

In spite of these obstacles, the representation of Afro-Americans stirring the entertainment stew was overwhelming at the turn of the century.

The Whitman Sisters

The Whitman Sisters, Mabel-Essie-Alberta-, and "Baby" Alice, comprised the family of female black entertainers who owned and produced their own performing company, which traveled across the United States from 1900 to 1943, playing in all major cities becoming the longest running and highest paid act on the Dudley and TOBA circuits. They became a crucible of dance talent in black vaudeville. They were called the greatest incubator of black dancing talent, and their star dancer youngest sister Alice was called "the queen of tap." She was considered the finest woman tap dancer of the 1920's and 30's. In 1889 Mabel, Essie, and Alberta formed "The Whitman Sister's Comedy Company" and toured all the leading Southern houses, playing to black and white audiences which at the time was unprecedented. In 1904 The Whitman Sister's New Orleans Troubadours was formed, and Mabel Whitman became one of the first black women to manage and continually book her own company in leading Southern houses. Refusing to follow the set pattern of segregated seating by having whites in the auditorium and blacks in the balcony, the Whitman sisters insisted upon having blacks being allowed in the parquet and dress circle sections of the theater, although spectators were probably still grouped together by race. In 1910 she organized "Mabel Whitman and the Dixie Boys" and toured the country and Europe. Her sister, Alberta, toured the U.S. circuit too as "Bert Whitman and her Three Sunbeams" to great acclaim. By 1914 Mabel Whitman had consolidated the family talent into the fastest paced show in African American vaudeville.

Williams & Walker were headliners in New York. Other producer-performers S.H Dudley, Salem Tutt Whitney, J. Homer Tutt, J. Leubrie Hill, Billy King, Frank Montgomery, William Benbow, and Irvin Miller headed and produced road show that played in black and white theaters from New York to Jacksonville Fla.---from Chicago To New Orleans.

The U.S. census of 1900 listed a black population of 8.8 million, an increase of 18% since 1890. A little over 1 million blacks were attending school, and the literacy rate was about 46% for blacks over the age of 10 years. The census also listed 35,000 white professional showmen with about 92,000 musicians and teachers of music. No statistic for blacks was provided in that category.

However the statistics published in the U.S. Census Report of 1910 showed a black population of nine million, an increase of nearly 10% above the reported 1900 census. Approximately 1.7 million Blacks were attending school, and the literacy rate had decreased to 30% for all those above the age of ten years old. The census data also indicated that about 67,000 Blacks were employed in professional services, and for the first time, included numbers of Blacks engaged in some form of show business occupation. The following tables compares the number of Blacks and Whites in this occupational category.

COMPARISON OF BLACKS AND WHITES ENGAGED IN SHOW BUSINESS IN THE UNITED STATES IN 1910 (U.S. CENSUS DATA 1910)

CATERGORY	BLACKS	WHITES
Actors	1,279	26,877
Musicians and Teachers of Music	5,606	38,370
Theatrical Owners, Managers, Officials	93	11,209
Theatrical Agents	9	2,135
Spiritualist,Fortune Tellers, Hypnosis	100	1,482
Keepers of Pleasure Resorts, Racetracks	54	5,638
Turfmen and Sportsmen	541	5,537
Total	7,682	91,248

This data indicates that by 1910 blacks had made a remarkable advance in Show business compared to 1900 when there were no statistics available.

MEDICINE SHOWS, GILLIES, and CARNIVALS

As the minstrel show was being ushered out of the American entertainment arena and stock companies began to grow and flourish in urban areas, a less sophisticated, yet unique theatrical expression, was being escorted in other parts of the country: the "traveling shows," the medicine shows, the gillies, and carnivals."

These unique shows experimented with new visions of creativity, giving the Afro-American performers of this genre an ingenious workout. Still waging a valiant war against the ugly arm of racism, and "Jim Crow" laws, African Americans performers were able to forge a measure of success through these avenues of expression.

The lack of interest and the usage of worn out materials and routines were the last nail in the minstrel show coffin. The stories found in the minstrel shows were outdated, and the appeal had diminished. The country was thirsty for a different flavor in the entertainment realm, and the creation of the medicine show satisfied that thirst. As America continued to grow and become curious about quick fixes and newly discovered miracles, the medicine show was born.

These types of shows were considered the introduction to touring circuits for many performers. The show was very simple and lacked the finesse of other touring shows of this time, yet it was an important and significant step in the growth of African American (vaudeville) musical theater history.

The comic genius, Pigmeat Markham, who received his taste of the entertainment touring circuit with the traveling medicine shows, sums up his experience as equivalent to the educational system.

"Show business and it's opportunities for African American performers was like going to school. You started out in a traveling medicine show, which was considered equivalent to kindergarten where your talent didn't have to be that great." (Jazz, pg. 108)

The traveling medicine shows were popular because they centered on the promise of providing the audience with a miracle medicine to cure anything from a colic baby to an average case of consumption. Of course, the miracle was nothing more than ordinary salt mixed with kitchen spices. As Pigmeat Markham recalls the ingredients in a fast selling medicine show remedy as nothing more than Epson salt and coloring.

As these shows traveled through the rural towns, the medicines carried impressive names such as "Kickapoo snake Oil," which added an air of mystique. Yet the main attraction was the black entertainment, which captivated the vast audiences. Medicine shows varied in size from a one to two man show going from door to door, to a show employing ten or more. The average show was a small show doing one nighters, stopping wherever they could find an audience. Traveling via wagon, the medicine show team would set up camp on sidewalks, open air fields or any strategic place which could catch the eye of the bystanders. First the dancers, accompanied by a musician, more often a banjo player, would excite the crowd with extremely agile and whimsical dancing. After the local townspeople were amused and delighted, "the doctor," would enter with his phenomenal medicine, preaching of its supernatural curing abilities. During this mesmerizing speech, the dancers would double as the doctor's assistants and sell the medicine to the captivated audience. However, a large success of the financial income was heavily attributed to the entertainers' ability to draw a crowd. Consequently, many African Americans traveling with medicine shows developed many outlandish dances to meet their audiences. This experience was a lesson in inventiveness and molded many performers with rare talent into polished acts. Even though the pay was not always good, and sometimes the performers were left stranded when the "doctor's" funds came up a little short, the medicine shows helped the African American performer find a forum of creative expression.

THE GILLIES

As an African American performer traveling with the medicine shows, it was considered a significant achievement when picked up by a gilly show, another traveling unit. The gilly shows offered the African American performer steady work, an increase in pay and a show with more spectacles than the medicine. Many African American performers on the gilly shows could earn as much as $15.00 a week, which was a huge financial step from the medicine shows. Still traveling from town to town but on special trucks known as gillies, these shows offered their audiences an array of entertainment, which included the ferris wheel and merry-go-round rides, games of chance, and tents containing human freak shows. Unlike the medicine shows, the African American performers' talents had to include singing and comedy, as well as dancing. Many African American performers aspired to move into the gilly shows for the special added attraction: the Jig Top. This tent was the exclusive African American entertainment haven where they created characters, dances and skits. The Jig Top afforded African American performers a chance to conceive and perform their own content, similar to the stock companies. This was a new phenomenon in African American entertainment history, and the performers exhibited their talents in a captivating and matchless manner. The show's structure consisted of beautiful chorus lines of three to four dancers, which led to a comedy team routine followed by songs and dances. The production began with a "barker" (usually light in complexion) announcing the lineup found in the Jig Top.

Leonard Reed, a famous dancer and creator of "the shim sham shimmy" served as a barker for a popular carnival, provides a first hand account of the job.

"They called the black show in a carnival the jig top. I became a barker for it because of my light complexion, and because I stood out. I stood in a box and called everyone around. I'd been given a speech..."ladies and gentlemen, gather up closer I've got a colossal collection of cannibalistic curiousities on on the inside. I tell you what I'm gonna do, you pay one quarter of of a dollar, twenty five cents....that's what they told me to say, cannibalistic couriousities on the inside" Now doesn't that say something about the attitudes towards black people in those days" (TAP pg 41).

However, the showstopper was always the energy filled "Eph and Dinah" routine. The skits premise was centered on a wedding anniversary of an old elderly couple. As the couple, Eph and Dinah, enters the stage, which is dressed as a plantation, they can barely walk across the floor because of the ailments of old age. As the rhythmic music fills the air, other couples begin dancing and trying to convince the old couple to dance a step or two. To appease the young crowd, Eph and Dinah strangle out a dance and faint from exhaustion. Yet Eph gets a burst of energy when he sees the eccentric dance, "the possum walk." This dance transforms old Eph into an aerobatics-dancing machine. Dinah, not to be outdone by Eph, introduces a sea of twirls, twists and turns to the dance. The crowd is brought to its feet in sheer ecstasy and bliss through this show. The African American performers were able to become one of the best attractions of the gilly shows and a pivotal point in the shows' success.

THE CARNIVALS

The more refined acts left the gillies for greener pastures: "the carnivals, even though the gilly shows provided the African American performers with a new voice through the jig top. Touring life was very taxing on the performers. The carnivals provided the African American performers with more exposure and decent traveling accommodations. Traveling via trains, better pay, and longer performance pay equated to a better opportunity.

Pigmeat Markham puts into perspective this phase of the entertainment ladder and its newfound opportunities.

"If you were a skilled performer with style you were likely to be able to get in a carnival; this was considered high school. College was the Vaudeville circuit or even Broadway where your act really had to be polished in order to compete on that level.

The carnival was also a refuge or a place to fall back on for established artist who were in between jobs. Ethel Waters from her autobiography, "His Eyes are on the Sparrow," describes the carnival "as always being a place to work for a blues singer with a hit record." The popularity of these traveling shows at the turn of the century helped the African American performer become a vital and significant player in the development of early American entertainment. In these shows, African Americans were frequently hired on their talents alone and was able to have the creative freedom to do anything that would attract an audience.

BLACK OWNER THEATERS----------(PRE TOBA)

As the urban stock companies, the traveling gilly shows, and carnivals were paving a new ground of theatrical expression for the African American performer, a new and bold initiative was being implemented----the ownership of theaters. Because of racial discrimination and an exhaustion from unscrupulous white theater owners, many African American businessmen and performers saw theater ownership as the most feasible solution. In 1901 some Chicago businessmen announced plans to establish a black theater in their city and gave the following reason:

> "It has long been a source of exasperation to the leaders of the colored society in Chicago that they could not secure box or orchestra seats in any of the white theaters, no matter how much they were willing to pay or how soon they got in line before the box office window. When they requested anything but a balcony seat it always developed that the show was doing sold out business, even if it was losing money in reality, and the colored person would be forced to take the balcony seat or no seat all. This fact has led to the plan of having a colored theater in Chicago, controlled by colored people and catering only to colored people (*The Ghost Walks*, pg. 208)."

African Americans realized that they would not be treated with respect and dignity while attending performances at the white theaters, even though they paid the same ticket prices as whites. African American journalist, Sylvester Russell, discusses this degrading policy of segregated seating in a letter published in The *Indianapolis Freeman* in 1904.

> "Dear Sir:
>
> I have been asked by people in Boston to express my opinion on the New York theater color line. The management of the New York theaters should have expected that some of the well-to-do colored families, of the greatest city in America, would expect to be accommodated on the lower floor to see "Williams & Walker" Some of the managers who are drawing the color line are Hebrews. No manager with Hebrew blood in his veins should draw the color line and expect the Americans to cease discriminating against the Jews at the exclusive hotel and summer resorts, when they are drawing the race line themselves. The New York managers who discriminate on account of color are greatly to be condemned. The public cares nothing about where a respectable colored person sits in the northern theaters, in this enlightened age. The thoroughbred white people would be delighted to sit next to the families of Bishop Derricks, who rode with a foreign prince or Booker T. Washington, who dined with the president, and converse with them (Sylvester Russell----*Indianapolis Freeman*, 1904)."

In September, 1905, the black owned American Theater in Jackson, MS was forced to open as a result of racial tension.

"The black owned and operated American Theater is formally opened with a performance of "The Black Patti Troubadors," who played to a packed house. The opening of this theater by Negro men was the result of racial discrimination by the manager of The Century Theater (white) in Jackson, who refused to book Negro troupes and made Negro patrons use the fire escape to reach the gallery (The Ghost Walks, pg 348)."

To place the wheels in motion with a cry for black theater ownership was Salem Tutt Whitney. Becoming increasingly exhausted from the harsh and blatant unfair treatment of white theater owners, Salem Tutt made an earnest plea to the African American businessmen to focus on purchasing theaters.

"Booker T. Washington has always maintained that the south is the natural field of endeavor for the colored man. No sober minded person will dispute him. Mr. Washington was hardly thinking of the theatrical profession when he made the statement. But a trip through the south will convince one that there has been no more rapid progress along any line than in things theatrical. Every town of importance has its colored playhouse, and for the most part, they are well attended. From empty storerooms and lots in the walls, there have grown many credible theaters with all the modern equipment, capable of seating from 500 to 1000 persons. New Orleans, Jacksonville, Norfolk, Richmond, Petersburg, and Newport Newsstand at the head at the present time. The outlook has been so promising that white theater managers are becoming interested. Jack Wells has brought or leased the Globe Theater in Richmond, which caters to colored people only. It's a sad fact that it is next to impossible to interest colored men of money in this sure thing venture. If a colored opens a theater for colored people and expends $2000 and does not make it back in the first week with a 9% profit he is ready to close down. There are exceptions of course, but they only prove the general rule. What is needed now is an organization of the colored managers, whereby they can exchange companies and talent and discuss things of mutual benefit. They must work in harmony. There should be a vaudeville exchange and booking house, and by all means let it be controlled by men of color. I am afraid that when the colored managers of the south finally stop "knocking" each other and awake from their lethargy it will be to find white men in complete control and reaping the benefits of our pioneer work. There is a great field for colored professionals in the south. While the wages are not so high as in the north, the expense of living is low and the jumps smaller. There is a crying need for producers. More men needed in the south like Bob Russell, Marion Brooks, Tim Owsley and others. I cannot think of a present intelligent man who can produce something original, who will give the public good clean shows and lift the moral standard of performances and performers. Everywhere the managers will tell you they can get the patronage if they could get the shows. Many good performers of the north would rather remain idle than venture south. To tell the truth you will be molested almost as quickly in New York, as in the larger cities of the south. You have practically nothing to fear, and the generous hospitality of the southern colored people will more than compensate for the ride in the "Jim Crow" car, and other salient reminders that you are a Negro (*Indianapolis Freeman,* Sept 6, 1910)."

On January 20, 1912 Sherman H. Dudley, a theatrical mastermind, followed Mr. Whitney's call with his bold stance against the established entertainment touring circuits by laying the foundation to implement the first African American touring circuit. As a successful comedian acquiring a high level of fame on the established medicine shows, Dudley removed his entertainer's hat and fashioned a new, successful entrepreneurial career. Dudley was no stranger to the entertainment circuit. He got his first dose of the entertainment bug as a medicine show performer in 1875. He then went on to organize the "IDEAL and GEORGIA MINSTRELS." He gained fame and popularity as S.H. Dudley & His Mule in 1904 when he led a mule on stage as part of "The Smart Set Company's production of "The Black Politician." However, with his strong entrepreneurial sense, he purchased several theaters from 1911 to 1913 in Washington D.C., including The MidCity, The S.H. Dudley, The Fairyland, The Foracker, and The Blue Mouse. Soon Dudley convinced other theater managers to join his circuit. The Dixie in Richmond, VA and the Globe in Norfolk, VA. These theaters became the original members of "THE DUDLEY CIRCUIT."

As a result of dealing with unscrupulous white touring circuits who limited his ability to showcase his wide range of talent and entrepreneurial skills, and also the vast lack of opportunity for African American entertainers, Dudley looked to other avenues to combat this deficit. Against the turbulent backdrop of the turn of the century Jim Crow segregation laws, Dudley made a public appeal, which would place African Americans at the reign of their own entertainment circuit and win financial and creative freedom for the first time in history.

Sherman H. Dudley

He meticulously revealed his carefully thought out plan focusing on the business aspects, which caught the attention of wealthy African Americans. This proclamation appeared in the *Indianapolis Freeman* newspaper in Jan, 1912.

Dear Sir:

I am adopting this method of putting up squarely to any prominent Negroes throughout the country who may be interested in theatricals, the following question, which I trust will be answered through your valuable columns. The things I wish to know are as follows:

How many colored men with money are willing to invest in theaters? The day is now ripe, the time has come, there is more profit in show business than in any other business you can invest your money in. If properly managed, why should you lose this opportunity? Give me ten theaters in ten cities and I will keep the doors open 365 days per year, and guarantee a success. I mean by this....if I'm provided with real theaters, planned and operated by colored men, and not backed by white men. These houses must be theaters. They are easy to get at this time. If you are in doubt, write me and I will tell you why. You don't have to build them. In nearly every city, there are theaters for lease. This is due to the passing of the "pistol drama" for whites, which has seen its last days, thereby leaving a vast amount of theatrical property practically valueless for immediate usage.

Ingenuity, experience and business forsight must be exercised in securing possession of this property without paying enough rent to buy the houses. Therefore, I insist if you are interested, write me and I will give you in detail my modus operandi. The following cities are available and the ones I most desire as a starter.; East Philadelphia, Pa...New York City---Baltimore---Wash. DC---Richmond Va---West Chicago, Il---Louisville Ky---St louis Mo,---Cincinati Oh,---Indianapolis In,---and probably Columbus Oh.

The most money in theaters has been made in recent years in the burlesque wheel. This is what I want to accomplish in the establishment of a chain of Negro theaters controlled and operated exclusively by businessmen of the race

(*Indianapolis Freeman*, January, 1912, Sherman
H. Dudley)."

A short two months after this letter appeared,
a poignant interview was printed in the *Indianapolis
Freeman* on March, 1912, which illustrated a more
socially conscience Dudley revealing the more personal
and passionate reason which motivated him to establish
the first black circuit. Shortly after his retirement from the
stage he discussed his dedication to his new self-reliant
venture.

The interview is as follows:

"I must devote most of my time to my enterprises
to make them a success. I know it is a hard task
and a great undertaking. Still I mean to make it
a success and with the aid of good, competent
surroundings and the loyalty of the vaudeville
performers, I cannot see anything but success. It
is only a matter of time, as the white theaters don't
care to play us. Someone has got to make a start to
find something for those hundreds and hundreds
of colored performers to do. I am going to find
work for them. The time is right and all we need
is a few more theaters like the Howard in Wash.
DC and The Grand in Chicago. I wish I could get
about ten theaters in ten leading cities, and we
would have what we have never had. There are
Negroes capable of playing from low comedy
to Shakespere's heaviest plays. This would give
them the chance. At present, my enterprise is in its
infancy, but it will grow. It takes time. I want the
management of all good acts in the business.

I can and will get them money and work. I
want all managers of real vaudeville to cooperate

with me. No honky-tonk halls, but high class houses. We have a few, and what we managers need and must do is to consolidate, and we will in time. Stop worrying about whom and what can I get next week for my show. I am going to spend all my time and energy to make it a success. I want the help of the performers and managers, the success will be guaranteed (*Indianapolis Freeman* ----March 1912)."

With that bold pledge of success, Dudley embarked on his quest of theater ownership. In 1911, Dudley catapulted his empire with the purchase of his first theater in D.C. His next theaters were located in Newport News, VA outside of D.C. By 1916 The Dudley Circuit consisted of over 28 theaters covering the south, east, and mid-west. The circuit made it possible for the first time that a black act could get contracts for eight months out of one office.

ACTS PLAYING THE S.H. DUDLEY CIRCUIT AND THEATERS OWNED BY BLACKS IN NOVEMBER 1914. From The Chicago Tribune Nov. 30, 1914

S. H. DUDLEY THEATER Washington DC
Martin & Motley Stock Co.
Lew Henry---Manager

HOWARD THEATER Wash DC
J Leubrie Hill's Darktown Follies
Andrew J Thomas----Manager

FORACKER THEATER, Wash DC
Dick & Struffin
George Tucker

FAIRYLAND THEATER, Wash DC
Drake & Walker Trio
Mr Ross---Manager

CHELSEA THEATER, Wash. DC
Special Pictures
D. Gentry---Manager

GREEN'S OPERA HOUSE, Richmond Va.
Nit & Tuck
Zel Bledseaux----Manager

HIPPODROME THEATER, Roanoke Va.
Davis & Green, Brown &Pinkey
W. J. Goulter---Manager

BOSTON THEATER, Lynchburg Va.
Whitman Sisters
C.C. Andrews---Manager

FORDS THEATER, New Burn NC
Bonnie & Samoura Clark
R. F. Johnson

DIXIE THEATER, Danville VA
Ricks & Talbert
J. H. Williams--Manager

NEW STANDARD THEATER, Phila. PA
Wiggins & Wiggins-Authur Allen
Butler & Allen-Butler & Johnson
Jones Ross and Pellelon Trio
J.T. Gibson

COLUMBIA THEATER, Phila. Pa
Massengale and Crosby
W. A. Donlevy ---Manager

VAUDETTE THEATER, Detroit MI
Kelly & Davis
E. L. Dudley---Manager

CROWN WINTER GREEN GARDEN
Three Cuban Nightingales
COLUMBUS OH
Billy Smith ---Manager

LINCOLN THEATER, Cincinnati OH
Watts Brothers
Marion Brooks—Manager

RUBY THEATER, Louisville KY
Reed's Georgia Troubadours
Wilholt & Collier –Manager

CROWN GARDEN THEATER, INDIANAPOLIS IN
Burton & Hock
Tim Owsley---Manager

CHURCH PARK THEATER, Memphis TN
Clark Co—Jones & Jones-Denslow & DEnslow
S. T. Beer---Manager

DIXIE THEATER, Danville VA
Anita Wilkins, Hugh Turner

Others joining Dudley on this theatrical empire quest was John T. Gibson of Philadelphia Pa., known as the "little giant." Gibson, unlike Dudley, did not possess a history as a performer, but was strictly an uncanny, excellent, businessman. In 1910 Gibson met businessman Samuel Reading, an owner of The North Pole Theater in Philadelphia. Impressed with Gibson's astute business savvy, Reading decided to take Gibson on as a partner, hoping he could help his ailing business. After an unsuccessful year together, Reading and Gibson's relationship suffered, and J. T. Gibson purchased the business from Reading for $800, thus beginning the J.T. Gibson vaudeville Empire.

After purchasing The North Pole Theater from Reading, Gibson turned it into an immediate success. But he didn't stop there. He next focused his attention on the much nicer and larger Standard Theater, which was a legitimate playhouse. It was at the Standard Theater that the Whitman Sisters were able to polish and develop their act into a fine traveling institution.

Post World War I prosperity brought wealth to J.T. Gibson, and the Standard Theater of Philadelphia was a veritable gold mine. Every week the receipts were well over $ 12,000. Many Stars of the twenties and thirties gained their first experience at the North Pole and the Standard Theater, including Ethel Waters, Bessie smith, Butter Beans & Susie, Buck and Bubbles, George Wilshire, and The Nicholas Brothers. Also the comedy team of Fairchild & Lovejoy gained experience at Mr. Gibson's theaters. Sandy Burns and Bilo and Johnny Woods, the ventriloquist, were a few others who kept the audiences dying with laughter. Gibson was an astute businessman that was always on the lookout for a good deal. He was also anxious to heed the call of Sherman H. Dudley for black theater ownership. And his empire employed black performers for almost 20 years before its demise.

About eight years after Mr.Dudley's circuit was created and Mr Gibson's acquisitions of his two theaters, E. C. Brown and A. F. Stevens organized The Douglas Amusement Company in 1919. The objective of the corporation was to raise capital for the construction of The Dunbar Theater on the corner of Broad and Lombard St. In 1919 Brown and Stevens also purchased the Quality Amusement Company thereby gaining control of The Lafayette Players Stock Company, and The Lafayette Theater in New York City. By the end of the year, the corporation either owned or controlled the following theaters: Dunbar Theater, Philadelphia Pa, Howard Theater, Wash. D.C., Avenue Theater, Chicago, The Putnam Theater Brooklyn, NY, The Perishing Theater, in Pittsburg Pa., as well as the Dunbar Theater in Philadelphia Pa.

In addition to The Lincoln Theater in Norfolk Va., this brought the number of theaters under Brown and Stevens to seven. E. C. Brown announced "that by years end nearly every large city in the country will have a first class theater catering to the race people which they can be proud and feel at home (Black in Blackface, pg. 309).

In 1920, Brown and Stevens announced ground breaking news for The Douglas Theater, a $500,000 theater in Baltimore Md. which would be the next link in the chain. However, Black audiences were not willing to venture uptown to the new Broad St. Theater. After only one year, it became a financial liability for Brown and Stevens. It was sold shortly thereafter.

In 1921, however, the fortunes of E.C. Brown's and A.F. Stevens' Amusement company took a downward turn. In April of that year, Quality Amusement Corporation withdrew from the Avenue Theater in Chicago citing bad business. A few weeks later Brown and Stevens sold The Dunbar Theater to J.T. Gibson. The Douglas Theater in Baltimore was the last piece of property sold by Brown and Stevens. Unfortunately, Brown and Stevens, it appears, were not as savvy as Mr. Dudley or Mr. Gibson, or maybe they were overly ambitious in their theatrical business pursuits. This fact is not known. However, it must be stated that they were doers, and they were willing to invest their money in their communities with the desire to change the condition of their fellow man by providing employment to so many African American performers.

Upon acquiring the newly built Dunbar Theater, J.T. Gibson also found it to be unprofitable. He found himself using profits from the Standard Theater to keep it operable.

After many successful years as a businessman and theatrical entrepreneur that built an entertainment empire, J.T. Gibson found his back against the wall, and in 1929 his theatrical empire came crumbling down. Real estate holdings were wiped out. The Dunbar Theater was sold, and finally The Standard went as well. Remarkably, Gibson became the owner of all the Black theaters in Philadelphia. However, the Great Depression caused them to be passed out of his hands ending what was the greatest era of Black theater and marked the downfall of Black theater ownership in any large degree in the cities of the east. The 1930's found Gibson just ahead of poverty. He died June 12, 1937.

It was the great stock market crash of 1929 that brought Sherman H. Dudley's theatrical empire down as well. He was able to hold onto a few of his original theaters, but that year found him selling his last theater to a white investor. The crash of 1929 virtually ended the great period of black theatrical entrepreneurship.

Although S.H. Dudley, J.T. Gibson, and Brown and Stevens were some of the first Black theater owners, it was Sherman H. Dudley who organized the first Black theater (vaudeville) circuit. The success of the Dudley Circuit gave birth to what became known as The Theater Owners Booking Association, also known as The T.O.B.A.

The "Theater .Owners .Booking .Association." also known as The "TOBA" Circuit.

Nothing smells sweeter than the aromatic scent of success, and after S.H. Dudley embarked on his Dudley Circuit, many white owners embraced this scent. The Dudley Circuit was more than a success; it was an awakening of the vast talent and financial rewards of an all African American touring circuit. Because of the fact that many African American performers never would have gotten an opportunity to showcase their talents with the white theater circuits, Sherman H. Dudley was able to expose them to a wide enthusiastic audience. In addition, Mr. Dudley employed hundreds of African Americans during a time when jobs were scarce with earnings at poverty levels. Many artists under the Dudley Circuit could get contracts for up to eight months out of one office, which was unheard of prior to his circuit. In doing so, it provided the performers with a high level of security. Furthermore, he reaffirmed the self-reliant spirit as proclaimed by Booker T. Washington. (a Dudley contemporary) "Lift yourself up by your own boot straps," only fifty years after the abolishment of the country's slave horror.

In addition to providing opportunities, The Dudley Touring Circuit created a radical social episode for white theater owners: "the all black night." This was the night African Americans were allowed to attend the all white theaters. On the all black night, African Americans attended in record numbers to view their peers as they displayed their phenomenal talents. The success of The Dudley Circuit made it more palatable for white owners to provide entertainment to the black population in their cities that were starving for entertainment. In doing so, it went against the racial code of segregation.

Unlike the minstrel shows and the unsophisticated medicine and gilly shows, the acts on The Dudley Touring Circuit carried an air of distinction because Blacks controlled their own performances. These performers were able to create and mold their talents without the embarrassing stereotypes beating their brows.

As The Dudley Circuit gained notoriety and financial success, it came under the scrutiny of other white theater owners who wanted to capitalize on the all black touring show phenomenon. As blacks and whites supported The Dudley Circuit in record numbers, white theater owners wanted to take advantage of this gold mine. Also white theater owners could book the African American acts at a much cheaper rate than their black counterpart. From that thought, The Theater Owners Booking Association, The TOBA, or as it came to stand for "tough on black asses" was nicknamed and born.

At first this new formation was a significant advancement for the African American performers because it exposed them to a new world of performance venues. The original officers of The TOBA were as follows:

Milton Starr, Nashville Tenn----President
J.J. Miller, Charleston S.C.-------Secretary
Sam E. Reevin, Chatnooga ,Tenn----Treasurer and
General Manager

The board of directors included:

T.S. Finley, Cincinnati, Ohio
C.H.Douglas, Macon GA.
Clarence Bennet, New Orleans
H. G. Hury, Birmingham Ala.

They were all influential theater owners located mainly in the South and the Midwest. This circuit was a carefully orchestrated organization, which was very protective of the theater owners from the outset. First, membership into the organization was offered to any theater owner buy purchasing three shares of capital stock at $100 per share. Members of the association automatically became recipients of a free franchise for life for the city in which it operated. They had access to a never ending well of African American talent at their fingertips. With such a lucrative business venture, the TOBA circuit grew to include over 80 theaters and could book Black acts for a full season.

THEATER OWNERS WHO WERE THE ORIGINAL
MEMBERS OF THE T.O.B.A 1920

H.J. Hury	Gay Theater	Birmingham Alabama
Milton Starr	Bijou Theater	Nashville Tennesse
E.B. Dudley	Vandette Theater	Detroit Michigan
E.C. Foster	Brooklyn Theater	Wilmington, N.C.
C.H. Turin	Booker T. theater	St. Louis MO
N.C. Scales	Layfayette Theater	Winston-Salem N.C.
M.A. Eightman	Plaza Theater	Memphis Tenn.
Charles F. Gordon	Star Theater	Shrevesport LA
J.J.Miler	Milo Theater	Charleston S.C.
T.S. Finley	Lyceum Theater	Cincinnati OH
C.H. Douglas	Douglas Theater	Macon, GA
Sam E. Reevin	Liberty Theater	Chatanooga Tenn
William Warley	Lincoln theater	Louisville KY
Bordeaux & Bennet	Lyric Theater	New Orleans LA
Clemmons Brothers	Lincoln Theater	Beaumont Texas
F.C. Holden	Liberty Theater	Alexandria VA
C.C. Schreiner	Pike Theater	Mobil, Alabama
Chintz Moore	Park Theater	Dallas, Texas
Lee & Moore	Lincoln theater	Waco, Texas
W.J. Stiles	Strand Theater	Jacksonville Fla
	Pekin theater	Savannah GA
E.S. Stone	Washington Theater	Indiannapolis ID
Lawrence Goldman	Lincoln theater	Kansa City MO
L.T. Brown	Dreamland theater	Muskogee Okla
	Dreamland Theater	Tulsa Okla

The TOBA brought to stage many of the now famous African American performers. It also initially became just as prestigious as the Dudley Circuit for African Americans providing work for hundreds of performers. Several

African American performers viewed the TOBA as a great opportunity because it provided work, and it afforded them the opportunity to travel. For many performers the only family they could make a claim to was other performers traveling on The TOBA.

Spending up to eight weeks on a tour caused many performers to develop a tightly woven support system where they "watched out for each other." Long time friendships developed as well as stubborn rivalries.

One such rivalry, amid mutual respect of talent, existed between Bessie Smith and Ethel Waters. Both women had totally different singing styles and were loved equally by their adoring fans, black and white. However, both ladies appeared at the same theater, the 81in Atlanta GA. Bessie Smith, being the elder statesperson, demanded that no one else was to sing the blues on her bill. Ethel Waters agreed to perform a dance number in respect to Bessie Smith's wishes. Still gaining notoriety as a singer, but not in the class of fame as Bessie Smith, Ethel took to the stage with her amorous yet tasteful "shake dance" and sang "I Want to Be Somebody's Baby Doll So I Can Get My Lovin All the Time." The audience went wild, but they still longed for Ethel Waters to belt out her Bluesy "St Louis Blues," for them to rock and sway by. The crowd became adamant with their demand, refusing to allow the show to go on with their uncontrollable yells and screams. To pacify the audience and prevent a riot, the orchestra struck up the chords for "St Louis Blues," and Ethel Waters satisfied their cries. The audience had unrelenting love for Bessie Smith's strong robust voice, which spoke to their souls, but they also wanted to hear the low, earthy sounds of Ethel Waters or "Sweet Mama Stringbean" as she was affectionately called. At the end of the show Bessie Smith imparted these words to Ethel Waters.... "You ain't so bad...it's only that I never dreamed that anyone would be able to do this to me in my own territory, and with my own people. And you damned well you can't sing worth a___ "

The TOBA was also responsible for bringing the phenomenal Peg Leg Bates, the famous one legged tap dance to prominence.

"I was with the Toba from 1922 to 1926. I came to NYC through the roof of the TOBA. During those years the TOBA, brought you to the large cities. TOBA was not only in the South, TOBA was in Cleveland, Pittsburg, and in Philadelphia. Like the Dudley Circuit the Toba played nothing but black performers. And through them brought me to The Lafayette Theater in New York, one of the most important black theaters in Harlem (Peg Leg Bates, Tap pg. 43)."

Another popular act on the TOBA was Earnest Baby Seals and his traveling troupe. The shows playing on the TOBA were tabloid editions of musical comedies, writes Clarence Muse, a freelance writer for The Pittsburg Courier. There were 3 shows given nightly, each about 45 min. in duration. The company for these reviews consisted of about 35 people. As mentioned Earnest Baby Seals and his wife Emma had their successful TOBA show. His wife Emma was a leading lady and sang the blues, as Baby Seals recalls.

"We started out with 18 in 1924 and gradually built up to 25 by 1931."

The show carried four sets of scenery and an 8 to 10 piece band.

"We were always discovering new talent on the road," says Seals.

Each year of its seven year successful run the show opened in Chatanooga Tenn, touring to Miami,

Willmington, Winston-Salem, Charlotte, Macon, and back again by a different route.

> "The Florida theaters for coloreds were fine," says Seals, "Palm Beach, Jacksonville, and Miami, and we did good business with an all colored audience."

> "If you don't make money on the TOBA, you were through in a week," says Seals.

His shows lasted an hour and fifteen minutes and was divided into eight parts, alternating comedy skits, chorus numbers, solo sketches, and always plenty of dancing. The fourth part featured the headliner and the last part was the finale with the entire company.

A lot of the comedy sketches were sometimes very risqué and wouldn't win any awards for high moral value, but the mostly adult audiences nonetheless enjoyed them anyway. As stated earlier family on the TOBA became very important to the performers. Stars like Bessie Smith were fortunate enough to purchase and travel in her own train car along the TOBA. Her entire revue, musicians, dancers, stage hands when needed lived, ate, slept and performed together on the TOBA. This was due, in part, to the "Jim Crow laws" as it related to restricted or separate traveling, which became a major issue in the South and other parts of America as performers attempted to get to one engagement to another. "Jim Crowism was so entrenched that in a Supreme Court decision of 1900 the "Jim Crow law" was upheld.

As this clearly demonstrates, there was a need for such accommodations on Bessie Smith's part, to insure safe passage and to avoid any disruption in the schedule, if you could afford one. It was said that Bessie Smith was known for burning some pots, and her large Sunday meals were an eagerly awaited treat at the end of a grueling week.

As stated earlier, comedy skits were very important to the success of a Toba show, and the need to have an expert comedian was equally important. White performers who gained fame and fortune later used a large number of these comedy sketches that were created by African American performers.

COMEDY SKITS FOUND IN BLACK VAUDEVILLE

THE BROKEN DIALOGUE

(Stevens and Stewart pantomime getting into a car. Stevens has trouble starting the car. Stewart releases the choke and the car starts. Stevens is constantly waving to friends outside the car as he drives down the street. Stewart tries to stop him from doing this and tries to draw his attention back to the road. Suddenly they see a car and brace for the collision, but it's too late and they crash.

STEWART----What's wrong wit it?

STEVENS----I just had it worked on..

STEWART----Who worked on it..?

STEVENS----The man who got the garage around…

STEWART----Oh no not him…the man you want is the man….

STEVENS----I had him, he the one that ruined it.

STEWART----Well I see you got plenty of water, but you sho you ain't out of gasoline?

STEVENS----Oh it ain't that, I think maybe….

STEWART----Naw it couldn't be that

STEVENS----Well it ain't much wrong wit it.

STEWART----What you need is some of them new kind of gadgets…de kind that you Buy…

STEVENS----I just bought some…

STEWART----Oh not them…I mean the kind that fastens where they fit. A whole dozen
            Will cost you about…

STEVENS----That's too much money…I can't afford that. I got to get something that cost
            No more than…

STEWART----You can't get em' that cheap…

STEVENS----We can get the car fixed up, for maybe around…

STEWART----No…what you need is a….
Both----a NEW CAR…..
STEVENS----You know one thing Stewart, if I get this car of mine fixed up, I just might take you and your gal out for a ride sometime.
STEWART----That'll be great…Can you make it on…
STEVENS----I'LL BE BUSY THEN….
STEWART----Well can you make it….
STEVENS----Well let's see, the best day for me is….
STEWART----That suits me, what hour?
STEVENS----Anytime between….
STEWART----That's a little early, but we'll be there…
STEVENS----Alright, I'll be seeing you.
STEWART----You know Steve, that why I likes talking to you
STEVENS----Why's that?
STEWART----Because we is good at..
BOTH----CONVERSATIONALIZATION.

.

BUTTERBEANS & SUSIE

(Susie hears a knock at the door)

SUSIE----Butter is that you messin around at the door?

BUTTER----Yeah it's me baby. I just come back from lookin for a job.

SUSIE----Well come on in here and tell me all about it.

BUTTER----Gladly (he tries to smooch her)

SUSIE----Hold on Butter, don't be smoochin all over me unless you got some money to put into this household. You ain't worked since we entered into this union of holy wedlock.

BUTTER----You mean "holy padlock"

SUSIE----Imma padlock your head if you don't stop messin with me man

BUTTER----Aw Susie, it's just that I feel like we is still on our honeymoon.

SUSIE----Honeymoon nothing. We been married for 15 yrs. You better forget about that moon and start getting up with sun and shine up yo'self a job

BUTTER----But…but…but

SUSIE----Ain't no buts about it.Cause this is one honey you ain't gon be moonin' over until you get me some money.

BUTTER----Now Susie, don't I go out lookin' for a job everyday? Alright,every other day or so. It's just that the right opportunity hasn't come along yet.

SUSIE----Opportunity? Butterbeans you wouldn't know opportunity if it smacked you in the mouth, and knocked all your teeth down your throat. And while you waitin for opportunity, I been workin' and slavin' tryin' to put food in our mouths. I have worked my fool self down to the bone, and we is at the point
of starvation

BUTTER----We may be starvin'(looking at her rear) but you ain't reached no crisis point yet.

SUSIE----(taking a swing at him) The point is I have married myself a no good, do nothin' good for nothin' zero

BUTTER----Aw Susie...you know I love you...

SUSIE----Well that may be so, but love goes out the window, when starvation comes through the front door. I knew I shouldn't have got myself hooked up with no geechie

BUTTER----Susie...I think I found me a job.

SUSIE----But now I know you married me for my job... job? What do you mean job?

BUTTER----I think I found me a job that will fit my station in life.

SUSIE----Station? You been stationary for 15 yrs.

BUTTER----Now there you go again Susie. Why don't you let me tell you what happened.

SUSIE----Alright tell me, and it better be good.

BUTTER----Well I went to the Inside-Out fabric company to see a Mr Out, who wasn't in so I waited for Mr Out to come in and when he did he said he had an opening for a trainee in the vat department.

SUSIE----Now what a minute Butter, is this another one of your lies?

BUTTER----Now Susie, would I lie to you?

SUSIE----Yes you would, remember I've known you for 15 looong yrs

BUTTER----There you go again woman, why don't you let me explain.

SUSIE----Explain

BUTTER---Now the job seems interesting and the pay is good, but I didn't take the job

SUSIE----What? What do you mean you didn't take the job?

BUTTER----Yet...yet...I didn't take the job yet. You see, I told Mr Out that I had to come in and discuss it with you first.

SUSIE----Discuss it? What's to discuss? You've been offered a job, you got a job. That's our previously discussed mutually agreed upon decision

BUTTER----But Susie, you don't understand what type of job it is.

SUSIE-----Whatever type, it's your type.

BUTTER---But Susie, wait a minute now. There's a problem with this job. You see if I'm hired as a trainee in the vat department, they would be trainin' me
to dye

SUSIE----Training you to die?

BUTTER---Yes my dear. That's why I wanted to discuss it with you first. You see I would be in trainin for 6 months learning how to dye, and after 6 months after I had learned everything,,,,I would have to start dying.

SUSIE----(scared and sadden) but Butter I don't want you to die. I mean I love you. And if takin' a job is going to kill you, then I don't want you to take the
job. It ain't worth dying for. Oh Butter please, please I beg you, don't take
the job (cryin)

BUTTER----(LAUGHING) Does you mean that sweetheart? Really? Truly?

SUSIE----Yes butter. If takin a job to earn some extra money mean you got to into into trainin' with all them vats (she realizes)....vat? Fabric company??/

Butter...you rotten skunk (as he tries to sneak away) You have pulled the wool over my eyes one too many times. You have done it again.

This time I have shorn the sheep. (she sings You Got To Get It Or leave It Out there)

EVOLUTION

(Stevens Enters the stage and begins miming taunting a monkey in a cage)

STEWART----Get away from that cage Steve, that monkey will grab you in a minute there
STEVENS----You ain't a-scared of monkies, is you?
STEWART----Yeah I'm scared of monkies.
STEVENS----Ain't no need to be scared of monkies. Why monkies is the closes thing to human folks.
STEWART----I wouldn't care
STEVENS----You learn about that in revolution. I suppose you know what revolution is.
STEWART----Yeah revolution is a war.
STEVENS----No, that's the ol' style revolution. I'm talking about the new style. revolution means that a man comes from a monkey.
STEWART----You don't mean to tell me you believe in that foolishness.
STEVENS----I didn't believe in it at first, but the more I sees of you, the more
suspiciouser I gets
STEWART----hey man, don't be callin' me no monkey.
STEVENS----I didn't call you a monkey.
STEWART----Well don't you done it then.
STEVENS----I wouldn't call you a monkey
STEWART----That's alright
STEVENS----I wouldn't insult…
STEWART----that's alright
STEVENS----The monkies. You see I don't know what you is, therefore I don't know where you come from. You too big for a monkey. By the way Stewart where did you come from anyhow?
STEWART----Georgia

STEVENS----I ain't talking bout that, I'm talking bout you generators. Where did you sprang from?

STEWART----I sprang from the cotton fields of Georgia

STEVENS----You couldn't, cotton fields don't produce nothing but cotton, and cotton is white

STEWART----All cotton ain't white

STEVENS----Bound to be white.

STEWART----Some cotton is black.

STEVENS----When is cotton black?

STEWART----When it's dyed

STEVENS----when it's what?

STEWART----When it's dyed.

STEVENS----Yeah but you livin' tho…What I'm getting at is your amsisters

STEWART----She didn't have none.

STEVENS----Yes she did.

STEWART----No she didn't

STEVENS----Everybody got amsisters

STEWART----All my amsisters was uncles

STEVENS----I ain't talking bout your amsister brothers. I'm talking bout your forefathers

STEWART----Now I ain't never had no four fathers (angry)

STEVENS----You did have fore fathers

STEWART----Man what is you talking bout?

STEVENS----Everybody had forefathers.

STEWART----If everybody had four fathers, there wouldn't be enough of em' to go

around. Let me ax you something?

STEVENS----Ax me

STEWART----Does you believe in re-incremation?

STEVENS----Does I believe in what?

STEWART----Is you a re-incremator?

STEVENS----Wait a minute. I ain't gon let you change the subject on me. I'm just gon fafta draw you a parallel so you can get my meanin

STEWART----Go ahead

STEVENS----Now take smoke

STEWART----Yeah….

STEVENS----What do smoke come from?

STEWART----A chimney……..

STEVENS----I ain't talking bout what it come thru. I'm talking bout what it come from, smoke come from coal.

STEWART----Smoke come from fire.

STEVENS----Alright then what the fire come from?

STEWART----A stove

STEVENS----What put the fire in the stove?

STEWART----The janitor put the fire in the stove, who you think put it in there

STEVENS----Evadin my question again, you know good and well that smoke come from coal. Smoke is coal used to be.

STEWART----Naw…smoke is heavy and smoke is light… there you is.

STEVENS----Smoke is light? Smoke is dark.

STEWART----I ain't talkin' bout the reflection of smoke, I'm talking bout the weight of smoke

STEVENS----You don't weigh no smoke

STEWART----Yeah you do….

STEVENS----Alright then, how much do smoke weigh?

STEWART----Well that's accordin to the size of the smoke, now a smoke like you
oughta weigh bout….

STEVENS----What …you callin me a smoke….?

SONGS THAT WERE PERFORMED IN
BLACK VAUDEVILLE

UGLY CHILE.....written by Clarence Williams. This song was performed in "Rollin on the TOBA"

STEVENS----man you is ugly
STEWART----man you is ugly
STEVENS----you some ugly chile
STEWART----THE CLOTHES YOU WEAR AIN'T IN STYLE
STEVENS----you look like that ape everytime you smile
STEWART----man I hate you, you alligator bait you
STEVENS----why don't you lay down and die
STEWART----you knocked kneeded
STEVENS----pigeon toed
STEWART----box headed too, there's a curse on your family
STEVENS----musta fell on you
BOTH----your hair is nappy, who's your pappy, you some ugly chile

HUGGIN and CHALKIN' written by Kermit Goell, and Clancey Hayes. Performed in "Rollin on the TOBA"

Oh gee, it's so nice to have a girl so big and fat
That when you kiss her, you don't know where you at
You got to take some chalk in your hand
And hug a way, and chalk away, to see where you began

One day I was a huggin, and a chalkin
And beggin her to be my bride
When I saw another fella , with some chalk in his hand
Comin round the other side

Comin round the other side
We was a huggin, and a chalkin, all day
(spoken) Baby I loves you to death, all of ya

HOP SCOP BLUES written by George Thomas

Ole New Orleans is a great big ol southern town
Where hospitality, lord it can be found
The population there, is very very fair
And lord the things they do
White folks even do it too\
They got a dance, and it sure is something rare
You got to glide, an slide, an prance, oh dance
And then you hop, stop, take it easy baby yeah, I say yeah
You never get tired of dancing that Hop Scop Blues
You fot to glide, an slide, and prance, oh dance
The Hop Scop Blues will make, you do a lovely shake
It makes you feel so grand, just walkin hand and hand
You never get tired of dancing that Hop Scop blues…..here
we go (he dances)
(adlibs while dancing……""I kinda like tis myself, "call
the police", "ya'll try this when yall go home, you hear")
I say, you'll never tired of dancing that Hop Scop Blues

ST. LOUIS WOMAN (BLUES) written by W.C. Handy

I hate to see the evening sun go down
I hate to see the evening sun go down
Cause mybaby he done left this town

Feelin tomorrow like I feel today
Feelin tomorrow like I feel today
I'll pack my bags and make my get-a-way

St Louis woman, with all her diamond rings
Pulls that mine of mine around her apron strings
If it weren't for the powder, and all that store bought hair
That man of mine wouldn't have gone nowhere, nowhere
I got the St Louis blues, just as blue as I can be

That man got heart like a rock in the sea
Or else he wouldn't have gone so far from me

ONE HOUR MAMA written by Porter Grainger

I'm a one hour mama
So no one minute papa
Ain't the kind of man for me
Set your alarm clock papa
One hour that's proper
And love me like I long to be
I don't want no lame excuses
Bout my lovin being soo good
That you couldn't hold out no longer
I hope I'm understood
I'm a one hour mama
So no one minute papa
Ain't the kind of man for me
(spoken) You better get some batteries

In the early 1900's as the stock companies were taking hold in urban black America, as J.T. Gibson and his Standard Theater in Philadelphia was becoming a mecca, as Sherman H. Dudley's Dudley Touring Circuit was ushering in the era of black theater ownership creating black entrepreneurs, and as the TOBA was beginning to emerge, another historic African American achievement was being accomplished with the creation of the Broadway production of "Shuffle Along."

LOVE WILL FIND A WAY

SHUFFLE ALONG, Inc. Presents
THE NEW YORK MUSICAL NOVELTY SUCCESS

Shuffle Along

"SHUFFLE ALONG," an African American musical revue, with music by Nobel Sissle and Eubie Blake, and written by Flournoy Miller and Aubrey Lyles, was the first Broadway musical written, produced, staged, and performed entirely by African Americans. The show opened at the Howard Theater in Washington D.C. on March 23, 1921. It premiered on Broadway in May 1921 at Daly's 63rd St Theater.

According to James Weldon Johnson, "Shuffle Along," marked a breakthrough for the African American musical performer and legitimized the African American musical, proving to the producers and managers that audiences would pay to see African American talent on Broadway.

Black audiences at Shuffle Along sat in the "orchestra seats" rather than being relegated to the balcony. "Shuffle Along" also featured the first African American love story.

Judged by contemporary standards, much of "Shuffle Along" would seem offensive. Some of the comedy relied on old minstrel show stereotypes. Each of the two main characters were out to swindle each other. Nevertheless, the African American community embraced the show, and the performers recognized the importance of the show's success to their careers.

"Shuffle Along," was one of the first shows to provide the right mixture of story, music, satire enticement, respectability, and romance to satisfy the black and white Broadway audiences.

Recording companies marketed all of the 18 songs from the show, including "Love Will Find A Way," and "I'm Just Wild about Harry," which became President Harry S. Truman's campaign slogan in 1948.

This landmark production strengthened the public interest in Black theatricals and marked a turning point in the history of Black entertainment in the United States. It introduced to the Broadway stage a Black chorus of partially garbed black beauties in the style of the white follies. Because of the show's popularity, the entertainment profession witnessed the presence of Black musical comedies to Broadway on a regular basis.

After "Shuffle Along" nine African American musicals opened on Broadway between 1921 and 1924. In 1928 the first edition of Lew Leslie's "Blackbirds," featured Bill Bojangles Robinson as the first black solo dance star on Broadway.

"Shuffle Along" is also credited with launching the Harlem Renaissance. An excerpt of the show, "the musical fight scene," between the two leading characters was made into a short film by Warner Brothers in the 1930's. Similar short films, featuring Miller and Lyles, were found in Warner Brothers' archives in 2010, where they had been misfiled. The titles are "The Mayor of JimTown" and "JimTown Cabaret."

As mentioned earlier, stars were created, first at J.T. Gibsons' Standard Theater, The Dudley Circuit, then an even larger audience on the TOBA viewed, loved and admired these acts. There were other acts such as Sarah Aikens, better known as "MOM's Mabley," Dusty Fletcher, who created the classic "Open the door Richard," Pigmeat Markham, who created "Here comes the judge" routine, and Hamtree Harrington who starred in some Black film shorts. Also touring the circuit was comedy team "Kid and Coot and the legendary pioneer tap dancer, Bill Bojangles Robinson, the young Sammy Davis Jr, with his father and uncle in The Will Mastin Trio. First the Dudley, then the TOBA, was the home to many female acts, such as Ethel Waters, Ma Rainey, Bessie Smith, Mamie Smith, the first African American woman to record a blues record, The Crazy Blues, by Perry Bradford, as well as the great Whitman sisters.

Unlike working at J.T, Gibson's Standard Theater, or working on S.H. Dudley's Dudley Circuit, work on the TOBA was very strenuous and exhausting. Performers worked five to six shows a day. Sometimes they would be cheated and only receive half pay. Managers would sometimes lie to acts to profit from the box office. Considering the times of the 1920's, it was unheard of for an African American to protest or even bring up an issue of being short changed. Only a few acts could possibly confront a theater manager with such issues, and not necessarily with any degree of success. Ethel Waters in her autobiography "His Eyes are on the sparrow" describes her confrontation with the theater manager in Atlanta. Because of this theater owner's power in Atlanta, he was able to prevent her and her troupe from purchasing railroad tickets, had her watched 24 hours a day to insure that she would not leave town before he confronted her, all because she "spoke back to a white man."

As we discuss the life and times of the TOBA, it is important to recognize the fact that there were some African American performers who were afforded the opportunity to play "white time" as it was called, or the white vaudeville circuits.

The Baltimore Afro-American Feb 6, 1926 provides this partial listing.

BLACK PERFORMERS ON THE WHITE THEATRICAL CIRCUITS

KEITH ALBEE CIRCUIT

Plantation Revue
Bryson and Jones
Gaines Brothers
Dixie Four
Jones and Peat
Harrington and Green
Joyner and Foster
Bill Bojangles Robinson
Glen and Jenkins

Four Chocolate Dandies

ORPHEUM CIRCUIT
Covan and Ruffin

WESTERN VAUDEVILLE

Harris and Holly
Tabor and Green

PANTAGES CIRCUIT
Chappelle and Stinnette
Sheftel's Revue

COLUMBIA CIRCUIT
Black and White Revue
Lucky Sambo
Monkey Shines
Rarin To Go
Seven-Eleven
Slidin' Billy Watson

These performers were the few that were able to some degree, escape some of the indignities and hardships faced by the majority of vaudevillians on the TOBA. Unlike the the Dudley Circuit, on the TOBA African American performers and troupes were always at the mercy of unscrupulous theater managers. Although the TOBA provided work for hundreds of black performers, many complained about the unfair treatment by theater managers. Before taking a show out on the TOBA, a show manager had to sign a contract, the terms of which were clearly in favor of the theater manager. In an article, which appeared in the August 18, 1928 edition of *The Pittsburg Courier*, Clarence Muse commented on the financial vulnerability of the show manager:

"At the beginning of the season, on or about Labor Day, six or seven week contracts will be issued to well-known producers and managers of shows. The term of the contract are carefully worded unlike any other theatrical contract in the world. But...if the show fails to appear, then pay and pay dearly even more than the contract will earn, as I will explain in detail. All of the contract is the party of the first part, meaning the manager of the theater, and the party of the second part, meaning the show, is only mentioned with no protection at all. For example, if it is a percentage date, and this is always the case, if the house does poor business, the contract will 50-50, must have 20 or more artist, names of the artist in the show must appear and if they fail to arrive a liability clause in the contract demands the show has damaged the theater manager in the sum of $1,500. But if the manager sees fit not to play you, he is not compelled to even notify you on a 6-day notice, and on liability, even if you appear, he doesn't care to pay you. There is seldom a show of this size that can earn $1,500 for their share unless it falls on a holiday week. And when a manager can earn an average of $1,500 a week on percentage, he will buy the show top salary at $1,200 take it or leave it. Now, note that for this $1,200 salary, with ridiculous road jumping, you must have at least 20 people, all excellent artist with a reputation, at least 8 chorus girls, and you must order and pay for at least $100 worth of lithographs, and share with all the newspaper advertising that the theater manager contracts for, and above all, $50 of the money must be paid to the TOBA as commission. The tremendous balance is for the salaries of the capable artist and with the average jump given by the circuit, it will leave about $400 to pay off all the artist.

Many theater managers have been branded all over the country by poor victims of the TOBA, as thieves, and all kind of unpleasant expressions unbecoming a theatrical and why....? Please keep in mind the average contract, and the terms therein. There is a fund set aside by this organization to take care of the initial cost of production at the beginning of the season, but they immediately encourage reputable artist to take out shows and we will advance you on your first date from $200 to $300 cash and your railroad tickets. Instead of taking this money back, as all circuit do a little at a time each week, they demand and collect every cent on the first date. This starts the pawn broker's department of the TOBA, and each and every week, you are hustling for a advance for the next date. Only every third contract is a guarantee date, and many managers want advance money, hence the sudden "bust out." The pawnbroker must be paid and the frustrated starving artist are left unpaid."

Today, one would ask, "Why would African American artists subject themselves to this type of treatment? We must keep in mind, during this period of time in our history, the performing arts was one of the largest areas of employment for many African Americans. To be able to make a living by performing on stage while getting paid, was the dream and goal for many African Americans who were struggling to survive. Unlike the Standard Theater, owned by J.T. Gibson, The Dudley Circuit, E.C. Brown and A.F. Stevens' Quality Amusement Company, the TOBA exploited this reality. Young and old African American artists jumped at this new opportunity.

On the black circuits, your act had to be polished, totally professional, and one that always made the audiences go wild. Black acts such as The Whitman Sisters and many others were able to make a career on the black circuits until the TOBA came along.

White TOBA owners were just looking for whatever they could get to capitalize on this new black entertainment phenomena. Some were talented, and those with little talent were eager to make money on the TOBA. From 1911 when Sherman H. Dudley, and J.T. Gibson purchased their first theaters, until the great depression of 1929-30, black musical theater under black ownership in America flourished.

In 1920 with the creation of the TOBA, things changed dramatically. As father time guided us towards the 1930's, America witnessed the last days of the TOBA. Several elements contributed to the decline of the TOBA.

Mabel Whitman of the famous Whitman Sisters viewed white theater managers as the greatest contributing factor to the decline of the TOBA. In an extensive interview with the *Baltimore Afro-American* newspaper, Ms Whitman offers great insight:

"The trouble with this game is a set of unscrupulous owners and managers seemingly have syndicated themselves together to stifle the progress along the lines of art and entertainment. They feel that any kind of show is good enough for a colored audience and their only desire is to have a comedian and a few half-naked girls on hand to keep the doors open enough for a colored audience. They insult the intelligence and prey on the Negro patrons. They say to themselves, that the Negro audience must have some place to go for their amusement, Instead of giving them the best possible talent, they palm off the worst as long as they can get a crowd. When the crowd gets fed up on that type of diet, they try to get a good show, and try to get it for the same money they pay for a amateur company which was made up over night. This is what a certain owner told me, and I'll name him, when and if necessary---"I have been losing money all year and I have to get out of the red on your engagement here. Therefore, I won't pay you what you want. You have a family company and you won't need money's because you all work and live together. Come in at my price or stay out". Well I stayed out! Cause I always had a home at The Standard Theater in Philly, and me and the "little giant" J.T.Gibson, always got along. And I stayed out, and I never will in this life pay a man who tells me I have to foot the losses he has suffered from bum shows. Let me give you some figures in this particular case. Years ago when I had smaller show, he refused to pay me a guarantee of $1,400. I went in on a percentage and took away $2,700 for my end of the receipts. The last time we played this house my cut for the week was $3,700. Then when he tried to get me this fall he offered me a guarantee of $1,600 instead of the usual percentage, and explained himself saying that I, Mae Whitman, had to make up for the bad weeks other people had given him. He offered me $1,600 for a company of 30 people, and it would cost me $490 in railroad fare, exclusive of baggage transportation to get there (excuse me if I'm not as calm as usual). What encouragement does a producer get out of that kind of stuff? How can you improve and develop your shows if there is no money available for a good show than for a misfit outfit? That is what an owner did here in Philadelphia. He even went to the individual members of the show in his house and ask them what their salaries was, offering as an excuse that he was about to produce a show and wanted to use them in it. At the end of the week he paid off the performers himself and paid the producer a musician's salary.

What does Mabel Whitman mean to one of this type? Does my name stand for anything with them? For no more than "Mabel jack Rabbit" With them it is an insolent "what are you going to do about it?" Take it or leave it. If these birds pay you a living wage they want you to guarantee that it will not rain or snow during the week you are booked with them. Something must be done and done quickly. But there is another picture, a bright and cheerful one. All owners are not in that category. In this game, there are men who appreciate your work and your worth. They will either pay you want you asked or not book your show at all until they feel they can do so. And they will pay you the same money or percentage for return engagements. They try to give patrons leading entertainment, and you always work harder for such managers. Believe me, twenty years of experience by Mae Whitman means something to them. In the west, in Pittsburg, Newark, these managers give us enough time to make out a season. They don't do this out of sympathy, they don't do it out of charity. True they are our friends, but they realize that we own more scenery, and more costumes than any other similar organization, thus reducing the house over head. They know we are money makers. They appreciate these things. That's why in the course of a season, we play from two to eight weeks with Mr. Gibson, and other high class theatrical men. Indeed, I spend so much time in Philadelphia that it is a second home for me. And now, you know what's the matter with show business (*Baltimore Afro-American*, Jan 19, 1929)!"

In another article, which appeared in the December 21, 1929 edition of the *Pittsburg Courier*, William Nunn commented on the decline of the quality of the shows on the TOBA. Mr. Nun lambasted producers for presenting shows of inferior quality in order to save money, expecting the African American public to be content.

"We don't blame the producer entirely. A couple of years ago this same TOBA, which is now hanging on the ropes, had some money to spare. Did they give one of our race producers a chance to improve their circuit? Nay..nay...nay.

They gave the money to Mr. (if you please) Jack Goldberg will-of-the-wisp theatrical promoter, and one of the smartest men in the game when it comes to looking out for Jack Goldberg. Goldberg, if this memory of ours is still hitting on all fours has been connected with more different theatrical ventures than any man around today. It was he who reaped the harvest from the original "7-11" company, a company which was made through the efforts of no less a group of principals than the hard working "Speedy" Smith, Mae Brown, and Garland Howard, a deluxe dancing combination, "Chink" the best oriental impersonator of his day, and a chorus, which, while not composed of high class beauties, stood as one of the best trained group of girl dancers this writer has ever seen. This was the show which took the old Columbia Circuit by storm for a year. And Goldberg had been connected with the Smith of "blues singer" fame and many others. Goldberg, we repeat was the man chosen by the TOBA to give a Negro public and abundance of what Negro public likes. His name tells his nationality. And what did Goldberg do? He started turning out shows at a rate of one –a- week. In Goldberg's estimation anything at all was good enough for Negro patrons of Negro houses. But the public failed to swallow Goldberg's "money bait" African American's wanted class and artistry and something new in the in the way of jokes. They desire a change from the old smut line of nauseating jokes. They wanted a degree of intelligence. They didn't favor or relish the ideas of a leading man coming to the front and splitting verbs.

They didn't relish the idea of girls appearing on stage in frayed, dirty costumes, and with run-over shoes. Why these condition prevailed, they did not know, but they did know they were not going to spend their money on something, and wishing they had not come.

From every angle –at the time Goldberg was given his chance, condemnation of the action of this body was heard. Why wasn't a Negro man of ability given the chance? Any number of good men could have been found who could have turned out shows, which would have satisfied.

Most prominently mentioned of the entire bunch was Irvine C. Miller, at that time overworked with the responsibility of trying to manage about five different shows. Miller's "models" "All Girls Revue," and "Red Hot Mamma," were his outstanding hits, but still he was in a position to get pretty girls, and he had solved the mystery of just what the Negro going to the theater, is crazy about.

Miller already had a nucleus of shows with which to start. He had corralled most of the available talent, and would have been able to get other high-class entertainers without a great deal of trouble. He appeared to be the logical choice. Since that time they have been slipping. Nothing of a remedial nature has taken effect. And the result now, is that the circuit, the actors and the managers of shows are mere puppets, suffering from the balking of an over abused public. We blame the TOBA. There is no mixture of sympathy in our condemnation. They had their chance and they have flunked it. Our advice is for the theatrical producers, who suppose to be real members of the TOBA but in reality are mere tools, to call a meeting of outstanding colored producers, if they could be obtained now, make them an offer, and back this offer with coin of the realm, if necessary (William Nunn---*Pittsburg Courier* December 21, 1929)."

As we draw attention to the life and times of African Americans performing on stage in the early 1900's, we simultaneously have to focus attention on the African American audiences as they waged a war against segregation and developed a new identity. As new entrepreneurial options were being exercised with the purchase and leasing of theaters by Negroes, the new mind set of producing and developing new theatricals serving and centering around Afro-American culture was also coming into focus.

The beginning of the blues being recorded by African American women sparked a new industry in the recording business, along with the advent of jazz as a new musical form. These elements contributed greatly to the creation of a new identity for African Americans new writings of writers such as Langston Hughes, Claude McKay, and Zora Neal Hurston. African Americans were becoming "in vogue" during this period of the twentieth century.

The audience's taste was developing and evolving to reflect the many voices of African American expression. These voices were being played out in a concentrated form in Harlem during the 20's.

Harlem became the mecca for this renaissance of African American expression, and it overflowed with black artists exploring their creativity. Freedom for African Americans overall during the 1920's was an elusive goal. African American entertainers represented a form of freedom for Negroes of the 1920's. However, most African Americans of the 1920's were relegated to subservience, barely being able to eke out an existence in segregated America. Entertainment at this time was employing more African American professionals than any other profession in America, according to the census reports of this time. This phenomenon in itself was indeed a new freedom, one, in which had many willing and waiting aspirants eager to leave poverty and segregation behind. Black creative expression held America enthralled during the 20's (refer to census chart).

As this new voice was taking shape, there developed a new intelligentsia among the creative artisans of the 1920's. The writers, musicians, dramatists, authors, along with the singers, dancers, and show people, exercised a considerable amount of freedom through this new creative expression, this new renaissance. This new intelligentsia, as it may be called, began to discuss the issue of art and its place as it relates to race. There was the struggle between art being used to advance the race and whether it should be used as a creative form of expression during this new renaissance. W.E.B. Dubois, James Weldon Johnson, and other writers of this renaissance kept this issue of art and its relationship to race issues at the forefront of discussion.

Coincidence with this issue of art as it relates to race issues was the actual race issue of Jim Crowism and lynchings. This was indeed a dark and violent time in American history as it relates to racism and violence perpetrated against African American entertainers and citizens on a whole.

One such example of the ever present danger took place in New York City during a riot in 1900 whereby an angry white mob attacked and attempted to kill George Walker of "Williams & Walker" fame, who happened to be headliners in New York. Ernest Hogan was also assaulted and had to flee for his life. This incident was reported by *The New York Journal* of that year:

"George Walker of the famous "Williams & Walker" was nearly killed by an angry crowd at 34th and Broadway. Walker was going uptown on a Six Ave car. At 34th St, the colored passenger was spied by the blood thirst crowd and before Walker knew what the trouble was a dozen men had jumped on the car and dragged him off. He realized that his life was in danger and as soon as he landed in a heap on the street, he jumped to his feet and sprinted up Broadway. More than 300 yelling men followed at his heels and caught him a block away. He was knocked almost senseless by a blow from the formost man of the pursuing crowd, and was soon trampled under the heels of the mob. He would have been killed had it not been for the timely appearance of a signal police who charged the crowd with his club and fought his way to Walkers side. The police carried him into the Marlborough Hotel where kind hands dressed his wounds. The wild, uncontrolled passion of the mob was best shown on Broadway at 12:30 o' clock this morning, when popular comedien and songwriter Earnest Hogan was chased like a wild beast with a pack at his heels. This rioting was wholly unknown to Hogan when he left the Cherry Blossom Grove, where he had been doing his turn as usual. A cry came from 44th and 8th Ave, and a mob of 500 men armed with clubs and stones surged over towards Broadway. Hogan was seen, "get that nigger" was the chorus. Hogan dropped his cane and started running down Broadway. The mob followed and for the next three minutes it was a life and death race for Hogan. At Broadway and 37th St Hogan was almost in the hands of his pursuers it would have been all over for him in a minute if he had not darted in an open door of the Marlborough Hotel Detective Madden, who ran from 35th St, stood at the door, and with a revolver kept the crowd back while Hogan was taken to the 36th St entrance and sent away from the crowd (*The New York Journal*, 1900).

Another incident occurred in new Madrid Missouri where the Georgia Minstrels Company was performing. Louis Wright, a trombone player of the company, was lynched for standing up to the horseplay of some white men in town. The company captured the entire ghastly event and the following story appeared in the *Indianapolis Freeman*, 1900.

We are now in the state of Illinois and doing great business, but under the strain of the most heinous crime that was ever perpetrated upon a traveling organization and most specially an organization bearing the reputation this show has. We feel greatly humiliated and embarrassed and our reputation has gone forever. We do not think the state of Missouri can pay for the damage done us, a body of innocent people. And it is well we were so clear of guilt. As luck would have it, no one here carries pistol, and this mob found none on us, but we had to suffer the same. If we had shot one white man in new Madrid there would not be one of us left to tell the tale, but certainly. Now presuming that the Freeman would be interested in the cause of justice, we hereby place the facts in detail just as they really happened.

To begin with the sad affair, the show entered the town of New Madrid MO. on the morning of Feb 15 at 2:30pm. We gave a street parade. Louis Wright, the victim, accompanied by another member of the company were on their way to the Opera House, when they were struck with snowballs fired by some young men of the town. They ask them to discontinue and were greeted with insulting names followed by another volley of snowballs, and it being slushy, naturally they could make them rather hard, hard enough to hurt a person if struck in the face or head.

At any rate, this last volley made Wright angry and he cursed them and continued on his way to the Opera House. Well the resenting of the uncalled for insults on the part of the white citizens aroused the anger that afternoon that a nigger had dared curse a white man. They claim that their intentions were to take the nigger that night after the show and whip him for daring to assert his rights and resent an insult offered by a white man. That a nigger had no rights in that town.

At any rate, the show went on along without interference until the curtain went down at the end of the performance. Then a crowd of men made a rush for the stage entrance that led to the auditorium, there being no stage entrance except a double door at the rear of stage used for loading and unloading baggage. They claimed that one of the young men received a scalp wound, and he came to the jail to try to identify the one that shot him, but failed to do so. They kept us standing up in a wet cell all Saturday night, and on Sunday we were taken out one by one to the court house, which was across the yard from the jail, to tell what we knew and who fired the shot. Our jury being about 32 of the best citizens in town and when we were brought before this body of law bidding citizens, the sheriff who ushered us into the this hall of justice, told us in their presence that "I can't protect you niggers any longer and you must tell who fired the shot, if not I leave you to whatever fate these gentlemen may decide.'

Well not a man in the company knew anything about a shot being fired by us, as we had not seen anyone fire a shot, and they failed to find a revolver or weapons of any kind among us, and we were very much of the opinion that the man (Hunter) received his scalp wound (if he received any) by one of his comrades during the excitement.

About the hour of midnight, Sunday Feb 16, one of these good citizens unlocked the door of the jail where we were and came to the cell and called Wright, telling him that the court was still in session and wished to get his testimony. Now this good citizen was not masked and neither were the good citizens that met him downstairs.

They hung the poor unfortunate young man from a limb of a tree in the front of a colored's family's door, not far from the depot, and left him until Monday about 10:o'clock. Monday morning they cut him down, they even took the rings off his fingers, at any rate, they put him in a box with his clothes on, just as he was, and shipped him to his mother, who lives at 3221 State ST., in Chicago. He was about 22 years old and a trombone player in the band. He was hanged because he dared curse a white man thereby resenting an insult the evidence of two young white boys who claimed that Saturday afternoon at the Opera House, while Louis Wright was in his short sleeves, they saw a handle of a revolver in his pocket, is a malicious lie.

This is a true and accurate account of the murderous affair. Not only Wright, but several other members of the company were shot and dangerously wounded. Against the backdrop of this racial hatred permeating America during this period, black performers persevered, and some prospered because of their unique gifts as artists and businessmen, as well as their instinctive desire to survive. They were able to forge out a legacy and build the foundation that this generation benefits from.

It should be pointed out that many forces came to play to damage and destroy black vaudeville. But none was more damaging than the stock market crash of 1929. This event affected not only The Dudley Circuit, J.T. Gibson's theatrical empire in Philadelphia, the TOBA, but also the entire business community of America on a whole, leading the country into the great depression, thus virtually destroying a treasured art form: "black vaudeville."

J.T. Gibson

Although the circuits disappeared, the indomitable spirit of the performers persevered. Most of the vaudevillians were forced into obscurity; however, there were many who were able to carry the flame of the tradition into other areas such as recording, film, and ultimately television.

After discovering this information about The first 60 Years of our remarkable, rich, entertainment history, I recognize that we performers of today owe a tremendous debt to those early artisans who persevered, in spite of hardships, and even death in order to leave us this legacy of artistic brilliance and entrepreneurial expertise, at a time in America where all odds of success were against African Americans.

THEATERS OWNED and OPERATED BY BLACKS 1910—1930

V===Vaudeville or Road Show
E===Equipped for shows, but showing pictures only
P===Pictures only
D===Dramas

LOCATION   THEATER   ORIGINAL OWNER

ALABAMA   (type)

Decater	MYKES—(E)	Sykes
Mobile	DIXIE PARK---(E)	?
Florence	BESSIE (P)	Mrs Reasle Foster
Sheffield	FIELDS—(E)	Elijah Fields
Opelika	DREAMLAND—(V)	?

ARKANSAS

Helena	PLACA—(P)	Mrs Eliza Miller
Hot Springs	VENDOME—(P,V)	?
Texarkana	?	Jason S. Douglas

DELAWARE

Wilmington	NATIONAL—(E)	Johns Hopkins

DISTRICT OF COLUMBIA

" "	HIAWATHA—(P)	Murray A Ryan
" "	DUNBAR—(P)	G. Rufus Byars
" "	DUDLEY –(V)	S.H. Dudley
" "	FORAKER—(V)	S.H. Dudley
" "	MID-CITY –(V)	S.H. Dudley
" "	RINE MOUSE—(V)	M Martin
" "	FLORIDA—(P)	Mr. Colfax
" "	MACEO—(V)	?

FLORIDA

Bartow	PICTURES—(?)	?
Jacksonville	AUSTIN—(V)	?
" "	globe—(V,P)	W.S. Sumter
Pensacola	LINCOLN—(P)	Dr. J. Seth Hills
		Frank Crowd
" "	ELECTRIC—(V)	M. Jacoby

GEORGIA

Athens	MORTON—(V)	William G. Garter
" "	PASTIME—(V)	?
Atlanta	PARADISE—(V)	Elijah Davis
' "	AUDITORIUM—(V)	S.L. Lockett
" "	ARCADE—(V)	?
" "	FAMOUS --(V)	J.B. Kelly
" "	PALM GARDEN (V)	W.G. Gray
Augusta	LENOX—(V)	J.A. Moffett
Brunswick	PALACE PHOTO PLAY	J.S. Buggs
" "	PEKIN—(V)	?
Columbia	OCMULGEE__(V)	W.M. Rainy
Decater	LUNA PARK---(V)	?
Macon	OLD DOUGLAS-(V)	C.H. Douglas
" "	WOVERLINE—(V)	Willie Braswell
" "	NEW DOUGLAS-(V)	C.H. Douglas
Savanah	PEKIN—(V)	W.J. Styles
" "	DUNBAR—(P)	Savannah Motion Corp.
Waycross	STAR—(V)	H.A. Hunter

ILLINOIS

Chicago	PEKIN—D,V)	Robert (Bob) Motts
" "	ROSE BIRD---(P)	W.C. Gates & Son
" "	STAR –(V)	Teenan Jones
" "	WESTERN—(V)	S.L. Owens
" "	DUNBAR—(V)	Dr. Richarson

83

" "	COLUMBIA—(V)	Robert (Bob) Motts
East St.Louis	OLYMPIC—(V)	King and Davis

INDIANA

Indianapolis	WASHINGTON-(V)	F.S.B. Stone
" "	INDIANA—(E)	Dr. O. Puryear
" "	AIRDOME—(V)	R.S. Geyer
" "	COLUMBIA—(V)	Hill Bros.
" "	TWO JOHNS—(V)	John Hubert
		John H. Victor

KENTUCKY

Lexington	PEKIN---(V)	Gray and Combs
Louisville	TAFT—(V)	Luther Edwards
" "	THIRTEENTH ST	Edward D. Lee
" "	PEKIN—(V)	Edward D. Lee
" "	NEW OLD FELLOWS	Edward D. Lee

LOUISIANA

Baton Rouge	BERNARD	?
New Orleans	L.K. MITCHELL-(P)	Luther K. Mitchell
" "	TEMPLE—(V)	E.S. Cheeberg
" "	BORDEAUX-(P)	Bordeaux and Camp
" "	PYTHIAN TEMPLE—(V)	King P Lodge

MARYLAND

Baltimore	RENARD---(P)	?
" "	DUNBAR—(P)	Brown and Stevens

MICHIGAN

Detroit	VAUDETT—(V)	E.B. Dudley
" "	SHOOK---(V)	Ben Shook
" "	UNIQUE—(V)	J.W. Hamilton

MISSISSIPPI

Greenwood	BIJOU—(V)	B.F. Seals
Jackson	AMERICAN—(V)	W.J. Latham
Mound Bayou	CASINO---(V)	Fred Miller

MISSOURI

St. Joseph	DUDLEY—(V)	Charles T. Phelps
St. Louis	BOOKER T.-	C.H. Turpin
" "	VENDOME—(V)	Mrs. Nora Warrington
" "	BARRETTS THEATERIUM	Richard D. Barrett

NEBRASKA

Omaha	CAMERAPHONE—(V)	?

NEW YORK

New Rochelle	NORTH AVENUE	Sydney B. Chase
New York City	RENASSAINCE—(P)	William Roach

NORTH CAROLINA

Charlotte	DIXIE---(V)	?
Concord	ALPINE—(V)	?
Durham	REX—(V)	Frederick Watkins
" "	WONDERLAND—(V)	Frederick Watkins
Rocky Mount	SANDY—(V,P)	Drs. P.W.& E.J. Burnette
Winston Salem	LAFAYETTE—(V)	W.S. Scales

OHIO

Cincinnati	PEKIN—(P)	Oscar Hawkins
" "	GAITHER—(V)	Edward Gaither
Columbus	EMPRESS—(E)	J.A. Jackson
" "	DUNBAR—(V)	J.A.Jackson and Ruby Williams

OKLAHOMA

Ardmore	?	Tobe Crisp
Guthrie	LYRIC—(V)	A.L. Sneed
Muskogee	DREAMLAND—(V)	Mrs. L.T. Williams
Oklahoma City	ALDRIDGE—(V)	Mrs. Zelia Beaux and Whitlow
Okmulgee	DREAMLAND-(V)	Mrs. L.T. Williams
Tulsa	DREAMLAND-(V)	Mrs. L.T. Williams
" "	PEKIN—(V)	?

PENNSYLVANIA

Philadelphia	DUNBAR-(V)	Brown and Stevens Later purchased by J.T. Gibson
" "	AUDITORIUM—(V)	Sam Reading
" "	STANDARD—(V)	J.T. Gibson
Pittsburg	LINCOLN-(V)	Harry Tennenbaum
" "	STAR—(V)	Charles Stinson

SOUTH CAROLINA

Bennettsville	LINCOLN-(E)	King & Covington
Charleston	LINCOLN—(V)	J.C. Cannon C.P. McClane
" "	MILO—(V)	?
Florence	PRINCESS—(V)	V.C. Brown
" "	ELITE—(V)	?
Rock Hill	BROADWAY-(P)	W.S. Alston

TENNESSEE

Columbia	LIVINGSTON-(V)	Livingston Mays
Jackson	PEKIN—(V)	William Blakely
Memphis	SAVOY—(V)	F.A. Barrasso

TEXAS

Beaumont	VERDUN—(?)	A.N.Adams
" "	LEE'S TENT—(V)	Edward Lee

Bonham	STAR—(V)	Charles Jordon
Dallas	PARK—(V)	Chinz Moore
" "	ELLA B. MOORE—(V)	E.B. Moore
Dennison	DREAMLAND—(V)	P. Woods
Houston	LINCOLN-(P)	Olum Pullum Dewalt
" "	AMERICAN—(V)	C.A. Caffey
Houston	PEOPLES—(V)	Frank Mckinsie
Rusk	QUEEN—(P)	Ed Conley
Temple	RINK—p)	J.J. Dawson

VIRGINIA

Alexandria	S.H. DUDLEY (V,P)	S.H. DUDLEY & Brown and Stevens
Hampton	HAMPTON-(V)	Hampton Theatre Inc. C.Tiffany Tolliver (pres) T. Green,(vp),Dr. D. Browning (sec) A.F. Brooks (tres) Major W.B.F. Crowell
Hampton	STRAND	" " "
Norfolk	ATTUCKS-(V,D)	Twin City Amusement Corp, Robert Cross Rufus Byars
" "	CLARK-(V)	F.E. Alexander
Petersburg	LORRAINE—(V)	William Williams
" "	S.H. DUDLEY—(V,P)	S.H. DUDLEY
Petersburg	RIALTO-	J.M. Wilkerson (pres.of a stock company)
" "	IDLE HOUR(V,P)	S.H. Dudley
Staunton	SUNNYSIDE—(V)	Mrs. R.I. Paunell

PARTIAL LIST OF BLACK ACTS PLAYING CIRCUSES, CARNIVALS AND FAIRS IN THE UNITED STATES 1900---1920

Pizarro's Tasmanian Troupe---acrobat

Bessie Coleman----stunt flyer

Maharaja----mystic and magician

Alphonso----showman

Sidney Rinks Society Circus---pony and trained mule show

Great Diamond circus Side Show—C.E.Warren (proprietor)

Robert Mills Anchor Concert Company—illusionist, magic

Billy Townsends Athletic Show

Princess Wee Wee—midget

Abnorma---Giantist

J. H. Dixon's Pit Show

Dave's Traveling Dance Orchestra

Watts Brothers---acrobats

Ira Green—acrobats

The Great Clemo—Contortionist, acrobat

Edwards and Edwards---wire walkers, balancers

Grey and Grey—Heavy weight jugglers, balancers

Billy English---hoop roller, Indian club juggler

DeWayman Niles---contortionist

Boyd and Boyd---contortionist, acrobat

Wells and Wells,--trapeze, horizontal bars, rings, 21ft high rigging

Gains Brothers—acrobats, high wire

Alie Johnson—"The Cat on The Wire", wire walking comedy

Coy Herndon---hoop roller, elaborate costumes, equipment

Lawrence Glover—wire walker

Dan Wiley----trick and fancy skater

Clows Gentry—rides down 100 ft incline dives into water

Amanzie Richardson---wire walker

Harry Wills---heavyweight fighter

ROUTINGS ON THE T.O.B.A. CIRCUIT, OCTOBER 1926

Baltimore Afro American, October 31, 1926

City,	State	Theater	Act
Chattanooga,	Tenn	LIBERTY	Marie & Clint,
			Charles Anderson
			Dudley & Byrd
			Snow & Snow
Nashville,	Tenn	BIJOU	Susie Sutton Co.
Hot Springs,	Ark	VENDOME	Roscoe Montella Co
Memphis,	Tenn	PALACE	Boisy DeLegge co
Shreveport,	La.	VENDOME	Williams and Brown
Dallas	Tx.	ELLA MOORE	Dusty Murry Co.
New Orleans	La.	LYRIC	Thomas & Breedon
			Green & Lang
			Jones & Chatman
			Fritz Jazz Lips Jr.
			Billy Arnet
Bessemer,	Ala.	FROLIC	Maggie Jones
			Sledge & Sledge
			Hampton & Hampton
Macon,	Ga.	DOUGLAS	Dudley & Byrd
			Prince and Connie
			Glasco and Glasco
St. Loius,	Mo.	BOOKER T. WASH.	Clifford Ross
			Long & Jackson
			Dooley & Robinson
			Bessie smith
			Sam Gray Company
Kansas City,	Mo.	LINCOLN	William Benbow Co
Galveston,	Tx	LIBERTY	Jackson & Rector Co